Esther Allen Howland

The Practical Cook Book and Economical Housekeeper's

Guide

Esther Allen Howland

The Practical Cook Book and Economical Housekeeper's Guide

ISBN/EAN: 9783744788878

Printed in Europe, USA, Canada, Australia, Japan

Cover: Foto ©Lupo / pixelio.de

More available books at **www.hansebooks.com**

THE
PRACTICAL COOK BOOK

AND

ECONOMICAL

HOUSEKEEPER'S GUIDE.

BY E. A. HOWLAND.

BOSTON:
ROBERTS BROTHERS, PUBLISHERS,
No. 143 WASHINGTON STREET.
1865.

Entered according to Act of Congress, in the year 1864, by
S. A. HOWLAND,
in the Clerk's Office of the District Court of the District of Massachusetts.

PREFACE.

Every young house-keeper, on leaving her maternal home for one in which she is to be the presiding genius, will often feel the need of some guide to which she can fall back upon in cases of emergency. Although she may have been well instructed by her mother or guardian, and have had considerable experience of her own, still there are so many new ways of mixing ingredients in the cookery and medicinal departments, that to keep up with the times, she often feels the need of a practical friend with whom she can consult; and the receipts here collected are for the assistance of such persons.

A large proportion of the receipts have been procured from experienced housewives, and no efforts have been spared to render each one as correct and as good as possible. The mode of cookery is such as is practiced generally by American house-keepers, and the receipts embrace all the various branches of the culinary art, from preparing the most simple broth, to making the most delicate creams and sweetmeats. The receipts are all intended to be written in such a plain manner, that the most unskilled need not err in attempting to follow the directions given.

In addition to the receipts for cooking, we have added Cookery for the Sick, Medicinal and Miscellaneous Receipts, which we trust will be found useful to the inexperienced. In conclusion, the writer would give her sincere thanks to those friends who have furnished her with their choice and valuable receipts; and to those into whose hands this book may fall, she would ask a fair trial of the receipts previous to passing judgment.

MEATS.

THE SELECTION OF MEATS.

This is one of the most important branches of household affairs. There is not one person in fifty who is capable of selecting good meats, if his butcher chooses to impose upon him; and as for cooking, I suppose every one will admit there is room enough for reform in this department, all the world over. I have therefore taken pains to prepare a system of rules and observations, by which any person of ordinary prudence and sagacity, can not only purchase good meats, but have them cooked properly.

1. BEEF.

If the flesh of ox-beef is young, it will have a fine, smooth, open grain, be of good red, and feel tender. The fat should look white rather than yellow; for when that is of a deep color, the meat is seldom good; beef fed by oil cakes, is in general so, and the meat is flabby.

In roasting beef, ten pounds will take about two hours and a half; twenty pounds, three hours and three quarters.

2. MUTTON.

Choose this by the fineness of its grain, good color, and firm white fat.

A neck of mutton will take an hour and a half, if kept a proper distance. A chin of pork two hours.

3. LAMB.

Observe the neck of a fore quarter; if the vein is bluish it is fresh; if it has a green or yellow cast, it is stale.

4. PORK.

Pinch the lean, and if it is young, it will break. If the rind is tough, thick, and cannot easily be impressed by the finger, it is old. A thin rind is a merit in all pork. When fresh, the flesh will be smooth and cool; if clammy, it is tainted.

A leg of pork or lamb, takes the allowance of twenty minutes, above a quarter of an hour to a pound.

5. VENISON.

If the fat be clear, bright and thick, and the cleft part smooth and close, it is young; but if the cleft is wide and tough, it is old.

6. BACON.

If the rind is thin, the fat firm, and of a red tinge, the lean tender, of a good color, and adhering to the bone, you may conclude it good, and not old.

7. HAMS.

Stick a sharp knife under the bone; if it comes out clean with a pleasant smell, the ham is good; but if the knife is daubed and has a bad scent, do not buy it.

8. PREPARING MEATS.

The foundation of all good cookery consists in preparing the meat, so as to render it tender in substance, without extracting from it those juices which constitute its true flavor; in doing this, the main point in the art of making those soups, sauces, and made-dishes of every sort, which now form so large a portion of every well-ordered dinner, as well, also, as in cooking many of the plain family joints,— is *boiling*, or rather *stewing*, which ought always to be performed over a slow fire. There is, in fact, no error so common among our cooks, as that of boiling meat over a strong fire, which renders large joints hard and partly tasteless; while, if simmered during nearly double the time, with less than half the quantity of fuel and water, and never allowed to "boil up," the meat, without being too much done, will be found both pliant to the tooth and savory to the palate.

For instance. The common and almost universal dish throughout France, is a large piece of plainly-boiled fresh beef, from which the soup—or "*potage*," as it is there called —has been partly made. It is separately served up as "*bouilli*," accompanied by strong gravy, and minced vegetables, or stewed cabbage. Now this, as dressed in the French mode, is always delicate, both in fibre and flavor; while, in the English manner of boiling it, it is generally hard and insipid.

To Stew.—This wholesome and economical mode of cookery, is not so well understood, nor profited by, in England as on the Continent. So very small a quantity of fuel is wanted to sustain the gentle heat which it requires, that this alone should recommend it to the careful housekeeper; but, if properly attended to, meat stewed gently in close-shutting vessels, is in every respect equal, if not superior, to that which is roasted; but it must be *simmered* only, and in the gentlest manner.

On the subject of *stewing meat*, the following directions may be advantageously adopted:—"Take a piece of boiling beef, with some fat to it, and a little seasoning, but without water, gravy, or liquid of any sort. Put it in an earthen jug, closely covered, and place that within a large iron or tin pot, filled with cold water, and lay it so near the fire as to keep a gentle simmer, without letting it boil. It will require several hours, according to the weight of the meat, which should be stewed until quite tender. It loses nothing, and will yield a large quantity of the richest gravy, as retaining the whole of its juice, and is decidedly the best mode of dressing that universal French dish—*bœuf-bouilli*."

To roast in perfection, is not only a most difficult, but a most essential branch of cookery, and can only be acquired by practice, though it consists in simply dressing the joint thoroughly, without drying up any portion of its juices. If this, however, be not strictly attended to, the meat will be spoiled, and the error cannot be rectified.

A brisk, but not too strong a fire, should be made up in good time, and care taken that it is sufficiently wide to take in the joint, leaving two or three inches to spare at each end, and that it is of equal strength throughout. The fat should be protected by covering it with paper, tied on with twine. The meat should not be put very near the fire at first, or the outside will become scorched, dry and hard, while the inside will be undone; but it should be put gradually nearer to the fire when about warm through, or it will become soddened; and the screen should be placed behind it from the commencement. The more the meat is basted, the better it will be when dressed, and the cook should not be sparing of her trouble in this respect. She should remove the paper a short time before sending the joint to table, sprinkling it with salt, and dredging it lightly with flour, in order to give it a savory, brown appearance; but salt should not be put to it before it is nearly dressed, as it would tend to draw out the gravy.

Meat which has been fresh killed, will take a longer time to roast than that which has been kept any time; and in warm weather, twenty minutes less time should be allowed for the roasting of a good-sized joint, than when the weather is cold. Time, distance, basting often, and a clear fire of a proper size for what is required, are the chief points that a good cook should attend to in roasting.

The joints of all necks and loins should be nicked before they are dressed. A piece of writing paper, cut as a frill, should be twisted around the bone at the knuckle of a leg, or a shoulder of lamb, mutton or venison, when roasted, before it is sent to table.

After the cook has taken up the roast meat, she should pour the fat from the dripping pan into a basin previously wetted with cold water. The next day she should scrape off the fine meat jelly, which will be found adhering to the under part, and put it into a suitable vessel for present use, as an assistant to gravies. The dripping should then be melted and strained. If required to be kept long, it should be strained into cold water, and taken off when cold in cakes, and these cakes laid in a dry place, between sheets of writing paper.

So much depends upon the taste of parties, in the mode of over or under dressing, that it is difficult to say how long a joint of meat of certain size should be roasted; but presuming that a good fire is kept up, and that the meat is intended to be well done, a piece of beef, say of twelve or fifteen pounds weight, should, in winter, be properly roasted in from three to three hours and a half. The common rule is, a quarter of an hour to each pound; but a thick joint, such, for instance, as a sirloin of beef, or leg of mutton, will require rather more time than the ribs or shoulder; and meat that has been hung for some days, requires less roasting than that which has been newly killed; mutton, somewhat less than beef; but veal, pork, and all sorts of white meat, should be so thoroughly roasted, as not to show any appearance of red gravy.

Some cooks recommend a method of roasting joints of meat in a slow manner, before a large fire, and placing them at a much greater distance from the fire, than in the common way, on the principle, as they say, "that it renders the meat more tender, and better retains the gravy." This, however, we cannot admit, for it does not retain more of the gravy, and it makes the flesh soft and insipid, or flabby, instead of imparting to it that degree of crispness which is caused by the ordinary mode. It also has the further disadvantage of requiring twice the usual time, and occasioning double the expenditure of coals.

To Boil.— All meat, for boiling, should be entirely covered with cold water, and placed on a moderate fire, the scum being carefully taken off as it rises, which will be, in general, a few minutes before it boils. This should be done with great care, as, if neglected, the scum will sink and adhere to the joint, giving it a very disagreeable appearance. The kettle should be kept covered. We cannot too strongly urge upon a cook the great advantage of *gentle simmering* over the usual *fast boiling* of meat, by which the outside is hardened and deprived of its juices before the inside is half done.

Pickled, or salted meat, requires longer boiling than that which is fresh. A fish-plate, or some wooden skewers, should be put under a large joint, to prevent its sticking to the bottom of the boiler.

To Broil. — A cinder-fire, or one partly made of coke and charcoal, clear of all appearance of smoke, is indispensable; and chops, steaks, and cutlets of all kinds, — if intended to be eaten in their plain state, — should be dressed after every other dish is ready, and sent up to the table *last*, so as to secure their being *hot;* **thus, it** may be observed, **that in** " steak-dinners," the second course **is always the best —as being dressed,** while the first is being eaten. The **gridiron should be kept so clean as to be nearly polished, and should be always warmed before the meat is** put upon it, as **well as greased, to prevent the steak being burned.** A fork should **never be used in** turning them, **but a pair** of steak-tongs.

To Fry. — The principle of this **art, is to** "**scorch something** solid **in oil or fat.**" To do this, **it is necessary that the fat should be in such a condition to scorch whatever is put into it**; for if the substance fried does not *burn,* it must *soak* **and become greasy.** After the substance is immersed in the fat, **the** pan may be removed a little off the fire, as otherwise the outside will become black before the inside is done.

When fried things are required to look particularly well, they should be done *twice* over with eggs and **crumbs.** Bread that is not stale enough to grate quite **fine, will not** look well. The fat you fry in, **must** always be boiling-hot **when** the meat is put in, and kept so till finished; a small quantity never fries well.

Suet. — When a sirloin of beef, or **a loin of** veal and mutton, is brought in, **part of the suet** may be cut off for puddings, or to clarify. **If there be** more suet than will be used while fresh, throw **it into pickle, made** in proportion of quarter of a pound of salt to a quart of cold water, and it **will be** good for any use when soaked in cold water a little.

If the weather permit, meat is much improved by hang**ing a day before it is** salted.

Boiling in a well-floured **cloth,** will make meat white. Cloths for **this** purpose should be carefully washed, and boiled in clean water before each using, and not suffered to hang in a damp place, which would give a bad flavor to the **meat.** The same applies to tape and pudding cloths. All kitchen utensils should be kept in the nicest order, and in a conspicuous part of the offices.

The more soups or broths are skimmed, the better and clearer they will be. In making these, as well as in boiling meat, particular care must be taken to take the scum off the *moment* before **the water boils,** otherwise **the foulness** will be **dispersed over the meat.**

Vegetables should never be dressed with meat, except **carrots or parsnips with boiled beef.**

Full-grown meats do not require **so much** dressing as young; **not that they are sooner** done, but they can be **eaten with the gravy more in.**

Hashes and Minces **should never boil, as their doing so** makes **the meat hard. The gravy** should **be thoroughly** made before **the** meat is put **in.**

Dripping or Clarified Suet, **will** serve as well as butter for basting every thing except fowls and game; for kitchen **pies,** nothing else **should be used.**

Mutton-Dripping **cannot, however, be used** in cookery, **as it is apt to communicate to every thing a taste** of tallow.

Seasoning.—**The** art of seasoning properly is a difficult one, which can only be acquired from experience. The cook tastes **her preparations instead of employing the scales; and, where** the quantities **are** indefinite, **it is impossible** to **adjust the** exact proportions **of spice or other** condiments **which it will** be **necessary to add in** order to give the proper **flavor; the great art being so to blend** the ingredients that **one shall not predominate over the other.**

In seasoning, though **the quantities of each ingredient may be as** accurately directed as possible, yet much **must be left to the** discretion **of** the person who uses them. **The different tastes of** people require more **or less of the flavor of spices, salt, garlic, butter, &c., which can never be ordered by** general rules.

9. TO ROAST BEEF.

Paper the top, and baste it well, while roasting, with its own dripping, and throw a handful of salt on it. When you see the smoke draw to the fire, it is near enough; take off the paper, baste it well, and drudge it with a little flour to make a fine froth. Never salt roast meat before you lay it to the fire, for it draws out the gravy. If you would keep it a few days before you dress it, dry it with a cloth, and hang it where the air will come to it. When you take up the meat, garnish the dish with horse-radish.

10. TO ROAST VEAL.

Be careful to roast veal of a fine brown color; if a large joint, **have a** good **fire**; if small, **a** little brisk fire. If a fillet or a loin, be **sure** to paper the fat, that you lose as little **of** that as possible; **lay** it at some distance **from** the fire, **till it** is soaked, then lay it near the fire. When you lay it down, **baste** it **well with good butter, and** when it is near done, baste it again, **and drudge it with a little flour.** The breast **must be roasted with the caul on till it is** done enough; skewer **the sweet bread on the back** side of the breast. **When it is nigh done, take off the** caul, baste it, and drudge **it with a little** flour. **Veal** takes much about the same time **in** roasting **as pork.**

LEG OF VEAL.

Let the fillet be cut **large or small, as best suits the number** of your company. Take out the bone, **fill the** space with fine stuffing, and let it be skewered quite **round**; and send the large side uppermost. When half roasted, if not before, put a paper over the fat; and take care to allow a sufficient time, and put it a good distance from the fire, as the meat is very solid; serve with melted butter poured over it.

11. TO ROAST MUTTON AND LAMB.

In roasting mutton the loin, haunch, and saddle, must be done as beef; but **all** other parts of mutton and lamb must be roasted with a quick, clear fire; baste it when you lay it down; and just before you take it up, drudge it with **a** little flour; but be sure not to use too much, for that takes away **all** the fine taste of the meat. Some choose to skin a loin of mutton and roast it brown; be sure always to take the skin off a breast of mutton. A leg of mutton of six pounds, will take an hour at a quick fire; if frosty weather, an hour

MEATS. 13

and a half; nine pounds an hour and a half; a leg of twelve pounds will take two hours; if frosty, two hours and a half.

12. TO ROAST PORK.

When you roast a loin, take a sharp penknife, and cut the skin across, to make the crackling eat the better. Roast a leg of pork thus: take a knife and score it; stuff the knuckle part with sage and onion, chopped fine with pepper and salt; or, cut a hole under the twist, and put the sage, &c., there, and skewer it up. Roast it crisp. Make apple sauce, and send it up in a boat; then have a little drawn gravy to put into the dish. This is called a mock goose. The spring, or hand of pork, if young, roasted like a pig, eats very well, otherwise it is better boiled. The sparerib should be basted with a bit of butter, a little flour, and some sage, shred small; never take any sauce to it but apple. The best way to dress pork griskins is to roast them, dress them with a little butter and sage, and pepper and salt. Pork must be well done. To every pound, allow a quarter of an hour; for example, a joint of twelve pounds weight, will require three hours, and so on. If it be a thin piece of that weight, two hours will roast it.

ROAST PORK.

Take a leg of pork; one weighing eight pounds will require full three hours and a half to roast. Wash it clean, and dry it with a cloth. Make a stuffing of crackers, powdered fine, with half a pint of cream, too eggs, a little salt, sweet marjoram and summer savory; cook about ten minutes. Put this in the deep incision made in the thick part of the leg. Do not put it too near the fire; it must be floured and moistened often with drippings, until it is done; then skin the fat from the gravy, add a little flour, and boil it well a few minutes. Apple sauce, or currant jelly, is proper to accompany all pork; also, potatoes, mashed squashed, turnips, pickles.

SPARE RIB.

If large and thick, it will require two or three hours to roast. A very thin one may roast in one hour. Lay the thick end to the fire; when you put it down, put into the vessel a pint of water and a table spoonful of salt. It **should be** floured and basted often with the drippings. The **shoulder, loin and** chine, are roasted in the same way. A **shoulder** is the most economical to buy, and is **excellent boiled.** Pork is always salted before it is boiled.

ROAST LEG OF PORK.

Choose a small leg of fine young pork, cut a slit in **the knuckle with a sharp knife,** and fill the space with sage and **onion, chopped, and a little pepper** and salt. When half **done, score the skin in slices, but do not cut deeper** than the outer **rind.** Apple-sauce and potatoes should be served to eat with **it.**

13. ROLLED NECK OF PORK.

Bone it; put a force-meat of chopped sage, a very few **crumbs of bread,** salt, pepper, and two or three berries of allspice over the inside; then roll the meat as tight as **you** can, and roast it slowly, and at a good distance at first.

14. TO ROAST A PIG.

Spit **a pig, and lay it to the fire, which must be a very** good **one at each end, or hang a flat-iron in the middle of** the grate. Before you **lay the** pig down, **take a** little sage, shred small, a piece of butter as big as a walnut, and pepper and salt; put them into the pig, and sew it up with a coarse thread; flour it well **over,** and keep flouring till the eyes drop out, or **you find** the crackling hard. Be sure to save all the gravy **that comes out of** it, **by** setting basins and pans under the pig in **the dripping** pan, as soon as the gravy begins to run. When **the pig is** done enough, stir the fire up; take a coarse cloth, with about a quarter **of a** pound **of butter in it, and rub the pig over** till the crackling is crisp, then take **it up. Lay it in a dish, and with** a sharp knife cut off the **head, then cut** the pig in two before you **draw out the spit. Cut the** ears off the head, and lay them at each end; cut the under jaw in two, and lay the parts on each side; melt some good butter, take the gravy you saved and put in, boil it, pour it into the dish with the brains bruised fine, and the sage mixed together, and then send it to the table. If just killed, a pig will require an hour to roast; if killed the day before, an hour and a quarter. If a very large one, an hour and a half. But the best way to judge, is when the eyes drop out, and the skin is growing very hard; then rub it with a coarse cloth, with a good piece of butter rolled in it, till the crackling is crisp, and of a light brown color.

Time, distance, basting often, and a clear fire of a proper size for what is required, are the first articles of a good cook's attention in roasting.

15. TO ROAST VENISON.

Spit a haunch of venison, and butter well four sheets of paper, two of which put on the haunch; then make a paste with flour, butter and water, roll it out half as big as the haunch, and put it over the fat part; then put the other two sheets of paper on, and tie them with pack thread; lay it to a brisk fire, and baste it well all the time of roasting. If a large haunch of twenty-four pounds, it will take three hours and a half, unless there is a very large fire; then three hours will do; smaller in proportion.

16. BOILED BEEF.

The meat should be well covered with water, so that the skim may be removed easily. Boil slowly and skim often. When beef is very salt, it should boil three-quarters of an hour; then take it up, throw away the water it is boiled in, and fill the pot with fresh water, re-place the beef, and let boil gently three hours. The round is the best piece to boil, then the edge bone; observe to take of the scum as it rises.

17. BEEF, A-LA-MODE.

Choose a piece of thin flank of a fine heifer or ox, cut into long slices some fat bacon, but quite free from yellow: let each bit be near an inch thick; dip them into vinegar, and then into a seasoning ready prepared, of salt, black pepper, allspice and a clove, all in a fine powder, with parsley, chives, thymn, savory, and knotted marjoram, shred as small as possible, and well mixed. With a sharp knife, make holes deep enough to let in the larding, then rub the beef over with the seasoning, and bind it up tight with tape. Set it in a well-tinned pot over the fire, or rather stove; three or four onions must be fried brown and put to the beef, with two or three carrots, one turnip, a head or two of celery, and a small quantity of water, let it simmer gently ten or twelve hours, or till extremely tender, turning the meat twice.

18. STEWED BEEF-STEAK.

Beat them with a little rolling pin, flour and season, then fry with sliced onion, of a fine light brown, lay the steaks into a stew-pan, and pour as much boiling water over them as will serve for sauce; stew them very gently half an hour, and add a spoonful of catsup before you serve.

19. BEEF-STEAKS BROILED.

The inside of the sirloin is the best steak, but all are cooked in the same manner. Cut them about half an inch thick; do not beat them; it breaks the cells in which the gravy of the meat is contained, and renders it drier and more tasteless.

Have the gridiron hot, and the bars rubbed with suet; the fire clear and brisk; sprinkle a little salt over the fire, lay on the steaks, and turn them often. Keep a dish close to the fire, into which you must drain the gravy from the top of the steak as you lift it to turn. The gridiron should be set in a slanting direction on the coals, to prevent the fat from dropping into the fire and making a smoke. But should a smoke occur, take off the gridiron a moment till the smoke is over. With a good fire of coals, steaks will be thoroughly done in fifteen minutes. These are much healthier for delicate stomachs than rare done steaks.

When done, lay them in a hot plate, put a small slice of butter on each piece; sprinkle a little salt, pour the gravy from the dish by the fire, and serve them hot as possible. Pickles, and finely scraped horse-radish, are served with them.

I have now given the most important receipts for cooking beef; the re-cooking requires skill and judgment which experience only can give. When well done, it makes excellent dishes, and is economical in house-keeping.

20. BEEF, COLD TENDER-LOIN.

Cut off entire the inside of a large sirloin of beef, brown it all over in a stew-pan, and then add a quart of water, two table spoonfuls of vinegar, some pepper, salt, and a large onion finely minced; cover the pan closely, and let it stew till the beef is very tender. Garnish with pickles.

21. BEEF, COLD STEAKS TO WARM.

Lay them in a stew-pan, with one large onion cut in quarters, six berries of allspice, the same of black pepper; cover the steaks with boiling water, let them stew gently for one hour, thicken the liquor with flour and butter rubbed together on a plate; if a pint of gravy, about one ounce of flour, and the like weight of butter will do; put it into the stew-pan, shake it well over the fire for five minutes, and it is ready; lay the steaks and onions on a dish, and pour the gravy through a sieve over them.

22. BEEF MINCED.

Mince your beef very small; put it into a sauce-pan with a little gravy, and a little of the fat of fowl or any other fat, season according to your taste, then let it simmer over a gentle fire till it is sufficiently done.

Boiled beef, when thoroughly done, is excellent to eat cold, as a relish at breakfast. The slices should be cut even and very thin.

23. TO STEW A SHOULDER OF MUTTON.

Bone and flatten a shoulder of mutton, sprinkle over it pepper and salt, roll it up tightly, bind it with tape, and put it into a stew-pan that will just hold it, pour over it a well-seasoned gravy made with the bones, cover the pan closely, and let it stew till tender; before serving, take off the tape, and thicken the gravy. It will take about three hours to stew the shoulders.

24. MUTTON CHOPS.

Cut the chops off the loin of the best end of a neck of mutton; pare off the fat, dip them in a beaten egg and strew over them grated bread, seasoned with salt and finely minced parsley; then fry them in a little butter, and make a gravy, or broil them over coals and butter them, in a hot dish. Garnish with fried parsley.

25. SWEET BREAD, LIVER AND HEART.

A very good way to cook the sweet bread, is to fry three or four slices of pork till brown, then take them up and put in the sweet bread, and fry it over a moderate fire. When you have taken up the sweet-bread, mix a couple of teaspoonfuls of flour with a little water, and stir it into the fat; let it boil, then turn it over the sweet-bread. Another way is to parboil them, and let them get cold, then, cut them in pieces about an inch thick, dip them in the yolk of an egg, and fine bread crumbs, sprinkle salt, pepper and sage on them, before dipping them in the egg, fry them a light brown. Make a gravy after you have taken them up, by stirring a little flour and water mixed smooth into the fat, add spices and wine if you like. The liver and heart are good, cooked in the same manner, or broiled.

26. MINCED MEAT.

Take cold boiled beef, removing all the bones and gristle, with a good proportion of cold boiled potatoes; chop them middling fine; fry three slices of pork in a spider. When the pork is brown, take it up, and put in the minced meat and potatoes; let it cook twenty minutes. Take it up in a covered dish, with the slices of pork placed on the top of a dish.

27. BROILED HAM AND EGGS.

Ham should be cut in thin slices, and broiled quick on a gridiron, set over good live coals. If the ham is too salt, soak it in hot water before broiling; if it is necessary to do this, dry it well with a cloth before putting on a gridiron. Fry what eggs you want in a part of good sweet lard, and a part butter; put an egg on each slice of ham.

MEATS.

28 BOILED HAM.

A ham, if dry, should be soaked twelve hours in warm water. Then put it into cold water, and let it simmer and boil five or six hours. It is best, when quite cold. Boiled ham is very good to broil.

29 PORK STEAK.

Cut them off a neck or loin; broil them over good live coals, turning them frequently; they broil in ten minutes. Sprinkle with salt and pepper when put into the dish, and add a small piece of sweet butter to every piece of steak.

30 TO BOIL A LEG OF MUTTON.

Cut off the shank bone and trim the knuckle; if it weigh nine pounds, it will require three hours to cook it. Parsley and butter, or capen-sauce, should be served with it; onion sauce, turnips, spinage and potatoes, are all good.

31. GOOD PICKLING FOR BEEF AND PORK.

Put in a pan or tub, five pounds of salt, three ounces of salt-petre, half a pound of brown sugar, for a joint weighing ten or twelve pounds, rub it well with the above mixture three or four times, letting it remain in pickle for a week; it is then ready for cooking. Half an ounce of pepper corns, or a few aromatic herbs, will vary the flavor.

Round of beef, edge bone, breast, flanks, or ox tongues, are the pieces generally salted. Small legs, shoulders, and belly of pork, pigs check and feet the same. Time your pickling according to size. For plain pickling, omit the sugar and salt-petre.

32. OBSERVATIONS ON CARVING.

In carving, your knife should not be too heavy, but of a sufficient size and keen edge. In raising it, no great personal strength is required, as constant practice will render it an easy task to carve the most difficult articles, more depending on address than force.

The dish should be sufficiently near, to enable the carver to reach it without rising, and the seat should be elevated so as to give command over the joint. **Attention** is to be paid to help every one to such articles as are considered best.

In helping fish, **care should be taken not to** break the flakes, which **in cod and fresh salmon, are** large, **and contribute much to the beauty of its appearance.** A fish knife, not very sharp, divides it best.

In carving joints, you must first truss your joint with taste, and take away any unsightly bone, to give it a goodly shape, more especially the neck, loin, or breast, of either veal, mutton, pork or lamb.

Roast ribs of beef, and sirloin, ought to be cut thinnish, following, as near as possible, the grain of the meat, which you can soon learn to do, by paying attention. Observe to let the knife pass down to the bone in the mutton and beef joint. A little fat and gravy should be served on each plate.

Salt beef ought to be cut thinner still. If out of a round or a sirloin side, cut it even. Cold meat requires to be cut thinner than hot.

Roast fillet of veal, to be cut as the round of beef, helping thin slices of bacon, or boiled salt pork, a little stuffing and gravy to be added.

Mutton requires to be cut rather thicker than beef or veal; pork the same.

In carving a leg of mutton, put one prong of the fork in the knuckle bone, holding it in the left hand, then cut five or six slices in a slanting manner towards you, dividing the first two or three cuts equally amongst all the plates. By this method you keep the meat full of gravy, each slice retaining its portion, and it is far better in an economical point of view, than cutting the joint across the center, as by this means all the gravy runs out, especially if the meat is over done. Haunch of mutton is carved the same, giving a slice of the loin, and one of the leg, to each guest.

Saddle of mutton should never be cut across the loin, if you study economy. Pass the point of the knife between the backbone and the meat, then begin at the top and cut as thin chops, in a standing position, each slice about half an inch thick, which **will give you a fair** proportion of fat and lean. By this **method, you cut** enough for ten or twelve persons; whereas, by the other way, you only get enough for four or five.

For leg of lamb or pork, proceed as for mutton, and for loin, ribs, breast or neck of either, proceed as above.

In cutting up any wild fowl, duck, goose or turkey, for a large party, if you cut the slices down from pinion to pinion, without breaking wings, there will be more handsome pieces.

33. MEAT BROTH.

Take four pounds of lean veal, beef or mutton, add four or five quarts of water, simmer it down to half the quantity, and an hour before it is done boiling, put in a little rice. Skim off the fat before it becomes cold.

34. BEEF OR MUTTON SOUP.

Boil very gently in a closely covered pot, four quarts of water, with two table-spoonfuls of sifted bread raspings, three pounds of beef cut in small pieces, or the same quantity of mutton chops; season with pepper and salt, and two turnips, two carrots, two onions, and one head of celery, all cut small; let it stew with these ingredients four hours, when it will be ready to serve. A little less than a quart of water is sufficient for a pound of meat. Soups made of fresh meats are best, but tolerably palatable soups may be made of the remnants of cold meats, especially if it contains many bones. The fat should always be skimmed from soup. The seasoning should be of salt, with a little pepper if it is liked; soup is more wholesome without the latter ingredient. To extract the strength from meat, long and slow boiling is necessary, and care should be taken that the pot is never off the boil.

35. SANDWICHES.

These are made of different articles, but always in the same manner. Cold biscuit, sliced thin, and buttered, and a very thin slice of boiled ham, tongue or beef, between each two slices of biscuit, is best. Home made bread cuts for sandwiches better than baker's bread. The meat in sandwiches is generally spread with mustard; the most delectable are those made with boiled smoked tongue.

36. DRIED BEEF.

Dried beef, sliced thin, is nice for tea, or venison dried is nice, sliced thin, or mutton dried and sliced thin is nice, together with good bread and good butter, and a dish of fruit, cheese, and a plate of cake of some kind. Some nice corned beef, sliced thin, is a substitute for dried; cold boiled ham, sliced thin, is a good relish, or cold tongue for tea. Some are fond of other cold meats of any kind, nicely cut thin. The manner of doing things is a great deal.

37. SAUSAGES.

Chop fresh pork very fine, the lean and fat together, (there should be rather more of the lean than the fat.) season it highly with salt, pepper, sage, and other sweet herbs, if you like them; a little salt-petre tends to preserve them. To tell whether they are seasoned enough, do up a little into a cake and fry it. If not seasoned enough, add more seasoning, and fill your skins, which should be previously cleaned thoroughly. A little flour mixed in with the meat, tends to prevent the fat from running out when cooked. Sausage-meat is good, done up in small cakes and fried. In summer, when fresh pork cannot be obtained, very good sausage-cakes may be made of raw beef, chopped fine with salt pork, and seasoned with pepper and sage. When sausages are fried, they should not be pricked, and they will cook nicer to have a little fat put with them. They should be cooked slowly. If you do not like them very fat, take them out of the pan when nearly done, and finish cooking on the gridiron. Bologna sausages are made of equal weight each, of ham, veal and pork, chopped very fine, seasoned high, and boiled in casings, till tender, then dried.

38. TRIPE.

After being scoured, it should be soaked in salt and water seven or eight days, changing the water every other day, then boil it till tender, which will take eight or ten hours. It is then fit for broiling, frying or pickling. It is pickled in the same manner as souse.

39. PICKLING.

Do not keep pickles in common earthen-ware, as **the** glazing contains lead, and combines with the vinegar. Vinegar for pickling should be smart, though not the sharpest kind, as it it injures the pickles. If you use copper, bell-metal, or brass vessels for pickling, never allow the **vinegar to cool in them, as it is** then poisonous. Add a tea-spoonful of alum and a tea-cup of salt to each three gallons of vinegar, and **tie up a bag** with pepper, ginger-root, spices of **all the different** sorts **in it, and you** have vinegar prepared **for any kind of** pickling. Keep pickles only in **wood or** stone-ware. **Any** thing that has held grease will spoil them. Stir them occasionally, and if **there are** soft ones, take them out and scald the vinegar, **and** pour it over the pickles. Keep enough vinegar to **cover** them well; if it is weak, take fresh vinegar and pour it on hot. Do not boil vinegar or spice above five minutes.

CUCUMBERS.

They **should be** small, green, **and of a quick growth, and** pickled, **soon after they are picked, to** be very nice. A very good **and easy way of pickling, is to put** them down with salt, having **a layer of the** salt to each **layer of** cucumbers; they should be **covered** with the salt **on the** top; let them remain till you **are** through collecting them, and the weather has become **cool. They** will have **a** shrivelled appearance when taken **out of the salt,** but will **swell out to** the original **size by being soaked in cold water** three or four days. **The water should be changed every day to freshen them. When freshened, turn off all the water, and scalded them in** spiced vinegar, with **alum to green** them; do not **let them** boil. They should be scalded a number of **times to** be made brittle. The following method is **more** troublesome, but it makes more delicate pickles:— Turn on boiling water, with **a spoonful of salt in it,** when fresh picked; let them remain **in it four or five hours,** then put **them in** cold vinegar, with **alum and salt, in the** proportion of a **large** spoonful **of** the former, **and a** tea-cup of the latter, **to** each gallon of vinegar. When you have finished collecting the cucumbers, turn the vinegar from them, scald and skim it, until clear, then scald the cucumbers in it, without boiling, adding pepper-corn and ginger-root, sufficient to spice the pickles. A few pickled peppers put into the jar with cucumbers, give them a fine flavor. Whenever scum rises on the pickles, turn it from them, scald and turn it while hot on to them; if weak, throw it away, and add fresh, with more alum and salt; if there are any soft ones, pick them out and throw them away. Pickled cucumbers need close watching during the warm weather, as they are very liable to spoil.

PICKLED TOMATOES.

Prick the small round tomatoes with a fork. Put them in layers, with plenty of salt, into an earthen vessel. Cover them, and let them remain two days in salt; then put them into a mixture of vinegar, that has been previously boiled, by adding to it mustard, cloves, pepper, mace, and a few slices of onions. Pour this into a glass jar, and put in gradually the tomatoes, shaking the jar to intermix the spices.

MIXED PICKLES.

An assortment of small vegetables in the same jar makes an agreeable flavor. Take small cucumbers, onions, cauliflowers, string-beans, tomatoes, barberries on the stem. Add a few whole cloves, cassia, and stick cinnamon; prepare the vegetables as before directed, and seal tightly. A little alum is very good to extract the salt taste from pickles. Too much will spoil them.

COLD SLAW.

Yolks of two eggs, a table-spoonful of cream, a small teaspoonful of mustard, a little salt, and two table-spoonsful of vinegar. If cream is not used, put in a small lump of butter rubbed in a little flour. Cut the cabbage very fine, heat the mixture, and pour it on hot.

CUCUMBERS.

"Who ever heard of cooking a cucumber!" we hear our readers exclaim. Try it, and tell your neighbors how well a poor man may live in the country. Take the cucumber, just as it begins to turn yellow, peel and slice it into salt water; drop it in cold water, and boil until tender. Season with salt and **pepper, mix** with batter and fry. Few can tell it from the egg-plant.

PICKLED OYSTERS.

Boil the oysters in their own liquor till they look plump, **then take them out and strain** the liquor; add to it wine, vinegar **and pepper, to** your taste, and **pour it over the** oysters.

A *Store-Room* is essential for the custody of articles in constant use, as well as for others which are only occasionally called for. These should be at hand when wanted, each in separate drawers or on shelves and pegs, all under the lock and key of the mistress, and never given out to servants but under her inspection.

Pickles and preserves, prepared and purchased sauces, and all sorts of groceries should there be stored; the spices pounded and corked up in small bottles, sugar broken, and every thing in readiness for use. Lemon-peel, thyme, parsley, and all sorts of sweet herbs, should be dried and grated for use in seasons of plenty; the tops of tongues saved, and dried for gratings into omelettes, etc.; and care taken that nothing be wasted that can be turned to good account.

Bread is so heavy an article of expense, that all waste should be guarded against, and having it cut in the room will tend much to prevent it; but, for company, small rolls, placed in the napkin of each guest, are the most convenient, as well as the most elegant. Bread should be kept in earthen pans with covers.

POULTRY.

40. CHICKEN PIE.

Joint the chickens, which should be young and tender,— boil them in just sufficient water to cover them. When nearly tender, take them out of the liquor, and lay them in a deep pudding dish, lined with pie-crust. To each layer of chicken, put three or four slices of pork; add a little of the liquor in which they were boiled, and a couple of ounces of butter, cut into small pieces; sprinkle a little flour over the whole, cover it with nice pie-crust, and ornament the top with some of your pastry. Bake it in a quick oven one hour.

CHICKEN PIE.

Boil the chickens tender, or nearly so, having them cut in pieces. Make a rich crust, adding a little saleratus, and an egg or two to make it light and puff. Lay it round the sides of the pan, and then lay in the chickens; between each layer, sprinkle in flour, pepper, salt and butter, with a thin slice of paste here and there. Then add the water in which they were boiled, and cover them. They should be baked an hour, or an hour and a half, according to the size of the pie.

41. CHICKEN POT PIE.

Wash and cut the chicken into joints; take out the breast bone; boil them about twenty minutes; take them up, wash out your kettle; fry two or three slices of fat salt pork, and put in the bottom of the kettle; then put in the chicken, with about three pints of water, a piece of butter the size of an egg, sprinkle in a tea-spoonful of pepper, and cover over the top with a light crust. It will require an hour to cook.

42. ROAST TURKEY.

Let the turkey be picked clean, and washed and wiped dry, inside and out. Have your dressing prepared, fill the crop and then the body full, sew it up, put it on a spit, and roast it, before a moderate fire, three hours. If more convenient, it is equally good when baked.

Serve it up with cranberry or apple sauce, turnip sauce, squash, and a small Indian pudding; or dumplings boiled hard is a good substitute for bread.

DRESSING.

Take dry pieces of bread or crackers, chop them fine, put in a small piece of butter, or a little cream, with sage, pepper, and salt, one egg, and a small quantity of flour, moistened with milk.

43. ROAST DUCKS AND GEESE.

Chop an onion with some sage, fine, mix with a lump of butter a tea-spoonful of pepper, and two of salt, and put it in the goose. Place it on the spit, dust with flour, when it is hot, baste with lard or butter. If it is a large one, it will require an hour and a half before a good fire. It may be stuffed with bread or potatoes. Ducks are dressed in the same way. For wild fowl, use only pepper and salt, with gravy in the dish.

44. BOILED TURKEY.

After the turkey is well cleaned, fill the crop with stuffing, and sew it up. Put it over the fire, and let it boil slowly in water enough to cover it; take off the scum. It should then only simmer until it is done. A little salt should be put in the water, and the turkey dredged with flour before boiling.

45. ROAST CHICKEN.

Chickens should be roasted in the same manner as turkeys, only they require less time. From an hour to an hour an half, is sufficient.

46. PIGEONS.

Pigeons are either roasted, broiled, potted or stewed.

Potting is the best way and the least trouble. After they are picked and clean, put a small piece of salt pork, and a little ball of stuffing, into the body of each bird. The stuffing may be made of one egg to one cracker, and an equal quantity of suet and butter, sweetened with sweet marjoram or sage. Baste them well, lay them close together in the bottom of the pot, merely cover them with water, put in a bit of butter, and let them stew an hour and a quarter, if young; an hour and three-quarters, if old.

Stewed pigeons are cooked nearly as above, omitting the stuffing. Being dry meat, they require good deal of butter.

To *Roast* pigeons, put them on a small spit, and tie both ends close. Baste with butter. They will be done in fifteen minutes.

To make a *Pigeon Pie*, put inside of every bird a piece of butter, and the yolk of an egg boiled hard.

47. CHICKEN SOUP.

An old fowl makes good soup. Cut it up; first take off the wings, legs, and neck, then divide it down the sides, and cut the back and breast each in two pieces; cut half a pound of pork in thin slices, and put it with the cut up fowl, into four or five pints of water; set it over a gentle fire, skim it clear, taking care not to keep it open longer than is necessary; add a cup of rice or pearl-barley, cayenne and black pepper to taste, a leek sliced, and potatoes cut in halves; if liked, a grated or sliced carrot, and a turnip cut small may be added.

CHICKEN SOUP.

Take two or three pounds of veal or vegetables, and one **small** chicken cut up; boil these in two quarts of water; cut up four onions or a leek; grate two carrots and add them to the **soup**; salt and pepper to the taste; skim it clear. Thicken the soup with a little batter of flour and water, with an egg beaten in.

48. SAUCES FOR GAME OR POULTRY.

Put into a stew-pan, and set on a slow fire, a quarter of a pint of white wine, a table-spoonful of vinegar, three table-spoonsful of olive oil, a bunch of sweet herbs, and spice to taste. Add to the whole some good gravy, and serve hot.

Melted Butter. — Flour the butter, and put it into a sauce pan with a little milk, stirring it carefully one way till it boils. Salt and pepper to taste. Another way is, make it with butter, flour, and a little water, with salt and pepper.

Onion Sauce. — Boil the onions until tender, changing the water occasionally to render them more mild. Strain, and mash the onions in a bowl, adding butter and salt. Warm up again, and mix the whole thoroughly.

Egg Sauce. — Boil the eggs very hard; when taken up, throw them into cold water; take off the shells, and chop the eggs rather fine; have ready your melted butter, into which throw them; heat it well and serve.

White Sauce for Boiled Fowl. — Melt in a tea-cupfull of milk, a large table-spoonful of butter, kneeded in a little flour; beat up an yolk of an egg with a tea-spoonful of cream; stir it into the butter, and put it over the fire, stirring it constantly; chopped parsley may be added.

FISH AND OYSTERS.

49. NEW ENGLAND CHOWDER.

Take a good fresh haddock or cod, cut it in pieces three inches square, put a pound of fat salt pork in strips into the pot, set it on hot coals, and fry out the oil. Take out the pork, and put in a layer of fish, over that a layer of onions, in slices, then a layer of fish, with slips of fat salt pork, then another layer of onions, and so on alternately, until your fish is consumed. Mix some flour with as much water as will fill the pot, (or use milk instead of flour and water, which is better ;) season with black pepper and salt to your taste ; boil it forty minutes. Have ready some hard crackers, which split, and put in about five minutes before you take it up.

TO FRY COD, OR OTHER FISH.

It is much more difficut to fry fish than meat. Lard or dripping is better than butter, because the latter burns so easily. The fat fried from salt pork is the best of all ; the fire must be clear and hot, but not furious ; the fat hot when the fish is put in ; and there should be sufficient to cover the fish. Skim the fat before laying in the fish. Cut the cod in slices, half or three-quarters of an inch thick ; rub them with Indian meal to prevent breaking. Fry it thoroughly. Trout and perch are fried in the same manner, only do not rub Indian meal on them. Dip in the white of an egg and bread crumbs, or dust with flour.

51. TO BROIL SHAD.

This is a very fine, delicious fish. Clean, wash, and split the shad, let it dry a few minutes, put it on the gridiron with the fleshy part up, and put it over good lively coals to cook ten minutes, then turn it in the same way you do salmon. When it is done, take it up, sprinkle on a little salt and pepper, and lay on two or three pieces of butter to moisten it.

52. TO FRY SHAD.

Clean the fish, cut off the head, and split it down the back; save the roe and eggs when taking out the entrails. Cut the fish in pieces about three inches wide, rinse each in cold water and dry on a cloth; use wheat flour to rub each piece. Have ready hot salted lard, and lay in the fish, inside down, and fry till of a fine brown, then turn and fry the other side. Fry the roe and egg with the fish.

53. SALMON.

When salmon is fresh and good, the gills and flesh are of a bright red, the scales clear, and the fish is stiff. When just killed, there is a whiteness between the flakes, which by keeping, melts down, and the fish becomes richer.

Salmon requires to be well boiled, and is very unwholesome when under-done; boil with horse-radish in the water, anchovy, lobster, or plain drawn butter-sauce; garnish with horse-radish and sliced lemon.

54. BOILED SALMON.

Run a pack-thread through the tail, centre of the body, and head of the fish, to bring it in the form of a letter S; then put it into a kettle with spring water, and plenty of salt. Cut three or four slanting gashes on each side of the fish, before making it in a form, otherwise skin will break and disfigure the fish; serve with lobster-sauce.

55. BROILED SALMON.

Cut some slices (about an inch thick); season with pepper and salt; wrap each slice in half a sheet of well buttered white paper: twist the ends of the paper and broil them over a fire of bright coals for ten minutes; serve in the butter with drawn butter or anchovy sauce.

BROILED SALMON.

Dried salmon is eaten broiled in paper, and only just warmed through. Egg sauce and mashed potatoes are usually served with it; or it may be boiled, or lay it in soak in pure water for an hour or two before boiling; rub the gridiron over with a bit of suet; lay on the salmon, shake a little pepper over and serve.

56. BROILED FISH.

Fish is exceedingly insipid, if sufficient salt is not mixed with the water in which it is boiled; about four ounces to one gallon of water, is enough for small fish in general; an additional ounce, or even more, will not be too much for codfish, lobsters, &c., and salmon requires eight ounces. To render the boiled fish firm add a little saltpetre to the salt; a quarter of an ounce is sufficient for one gallon.

57. SALMON, ROLLED.

Take a side of salmon, remove the bone, clean it nicely, and throw over the inside pepper, salt, nutmeg and sauce, with a few chopped oysters, parsley and crumbs of bread. Roll it up tight, put it into a deep pot, and bake it in a quick oven. Make a common fish sauce and pour over it.

58. FRIED SMELTS.

Take two pounds of good fresh smelts, wash and dry well; break three eggs; season with pepper and salt; beat them well together; dip the smelts in the eggs, and roll them in crumbs; fry them a bright brown; served with parsley or lemons to garnish the dish.

59. CLAM SOUP.

Fifty large, or one hundred small clams, will be sufficient. In removing them from the shell, carefully preserve the liquor, which should be strained, and to it add a quart of milk and water each; if the clams are large, cut each in two, and put them into it; set them over a moderate fire until the clams are tender (about one hour); skim it clear; put it to half a pound of soda crackers, broken small, or half a pound of butter crackers, rolled fine; cover the pot for ten minutes; then add a quarter of a pound of sweet butter, and serve hot.

60. OYSTER SOUP.

Mix three pints each of milk and water. Half a pound of butter crackers, or soda biscuit (rolled fine) should be added with a pint of oysters (chopped fine,) when the milk and water comes to a boil. Let it boil until the flavor of oysters is given to soup, and the crackers are well swelled; then add salt and pepper to taste, and three pints of more of the oysters, with a quarter of a pound of sweet butter; cover it for ten minutes more, then serve it in a tureen.

61. TO FRY HADDOCK.

If of a very small size, they may be turned round with their tails run through their jaws; but this cannot be done when they are large; they are, in that case, either cut in slices or filletted, and fried with crumbs of bread and egg.

62. BROOK TROUT.

If they are small, fry them with salt pork. If large, boil them, and serve them with drawn butter.

63. DISH OF FRIED COD.

Pick some dried cod in flakes, pour boiling water over, scald it once, then throw the water off; put some hot milk or water over, to which add a bit of butter; pepper to taste, and serve.

64. CODFISH CAKES.

First boil the fish, then take the white part, chop it fine with a chopping knife, add mashed potatoes, an equal quantity, and form them in cakes, with a raw egg or two, and a little flour; dredge the outside with flour, and fry in hot lard or drippings; garnish with fried parsley.

65. FRIED SHAD.

Scale the fish, cut off the head, and then cut down the back, and take out the entrails; keep the roes to be dressed with the fish, then cut it in two, and cut each side in pieces, about three inches wide; flour them, and fry in hot lard, in which put salt to taste. When the inside, (which must always be first cooked in any fish,) is done a fine brown, turn the other. The soft roe is much liked by some; fry it in the same manner; as also the eggs from the female shad; these last must be well done.

66. SALT MACKEREL.

Lay them in soak in plenty of clear water before using them, at least twelve hours, and fry, or broil them, or put them in a frying-pan. Cover with boiling water, and give them fifteen minutes cooking, then pour off the water; pepper to taste and serve.

67. FRESH MACKEREL SOUSED.

After having thoroughly cleaned them, boil them in salt and water until tender; then take them out, lay them in a deep dish; take of the water in which they were boiled, half as much will cover them; add to it as much more vinegar, some whole pepper, cloves, and a blade or two of mace. Pour it over hot; in two days it will be fit to eat.

68. BROILED COD.

Split a small cod from head to tail; cut the sides in pieces of about three inches in width; dip them in flour and broil; have some butter, pepper, and salt on a hot dish; lay the fish on this and serve.

Or, take the steaks, broil them in the same way, or with buttered paper folded around them.

69. FRIED COD.

Take steaks of about an inch thickness, dredge them with flour, and fry them in hot fat; or if a small one, cut it the same as for boiling, and flour it, or first dip it in the beaten yolks of eggs, and then in bread crumbs.

70. SALT CODFISH.

Put the fish in soak over night: tie it in a cloth, and boil in clear water; serve with plain boiled potatoes and drawn butter or egg sauce,

71. DRIED CODFISH.

This should always be laid in soak with plenty of water, at least one night before cooking; after which, scrape it well, and put it in plenty of cold water; let it boil gently; skim it; when done, serve with egg sauce over, or cut hard boiled eggs in slices, lay them over the fish, and serve with drawn butter in a boat.

72. STEWED SALT COD.

Scald some cod, scrape it white, then pick it in pieces, and put in a stew-pan with some butter rolled in flour; milk enough to moisten it, and pepper to taste, and let it stew slowly for some minutes, then serve hot.

73. TO MAKE A DISH OF COLD BOILED COD.

Take some boiled fish, chop it fine, pour some drawn butter or egg sauce over, add pepper to taste; warm it thoroughly, stirring it to prevent its burning; make a roll or any other form of it; put little spots of pepper over, and if you please, brown the outside before a fire.

74. EEL BROTH.

Clean half a pound of small eels, and set them on with three pints of water, some parsley, one slice of onion, a few peppercorns; let them simmer till the ends are broken, and the broth good, or reduced to a pint and a half. Add salt, and strain it off. It is very nutritious.

75. STEWED OYSTERS.

Strain off the liquor, put to it some milk or water, grate in dry bread, add a little pepper and a lump of butter, put these in a stew-pan and broil; then add the oysters. Let them stew but a few minutes, or they will be hard. Have ready some slices of buttered toast with the crust off. When the oysters are done, dip the toast in the liquor, and lay the pieces round the sides and in the bottom of a deep dish. Pour the oysters and liquor upon the toast, and send them to the table hot.

76. OYSTER SAUCE.

Beard and scald the oysters; strain the liquor and thicken it with a little flour and butter. Squeeze in a little lemon juice, and add in three table spoonsful of cream. Heat it well, but do not let it boil.

77. TO FRY OYSTERS.

Make a batter as for pancakes; put one or two oysters into a spoonful of the batter, and fry them to a light brown. Fry them in hot fat the same as pancakes.

FISH SAUCES.

Lobster Sauce. — Take a large, fresh lobster, carefully pick out the berries and all the inside, cut it small, make a sauce with a lump of flour and butter, a little milk or cream, a very small quantity of the essence of anchovy, a very little mace beat fine, and cayenne; then pull the rest of the lobster to pieces with two forks; add the sauce by degrees to the berries, and put in the lobster. Give it a boil, stirring all the time, and it is ready to serve.

Brown Sauce for Fish. — Melt some butter in cream, (instead of flour and water,) with as much walnut ketchup boiled in it as will make it of a nice light brown.

White Sauce for Fish. — Boil some cream, thicken it with flour and butter, then let it simmer till smooth; add a teaspoonful of the essence of anchovy to a tureenful, and, if it is liked, a little walnut or mushroom ketchup. For cod sauce, omit the anchovy and ketchup, and add a little ginger. If cream is scarce, use milk and the yolk of an egg.

VEGETABLES.

78. POTATOES.

Potatoes will not keep well in the cellar if exposed to the light. They should be placed in a bin, and covered with straw, and packed in barrels, with the tops completely closed against the light by old carpets.

79. COOKING POTATOES.

To cook potatoes in the best manner, is a great perfection in cooking. The following way is a good one. Take potatoes as equal in size as possible; wash, but do not pare or cut them; put them into a pot, the largest potatoes at the bottom; cover them with cold water, about an inch over; too much water injures them very much; throw in a spoonful of salt, and set it where it will simmer slowly for thirty minutes; then try the potatoes with a fork; if it pass easily through, they are done; if not, let them simmer till they are; then pour off the water, place the pot where the potatoes will keep hot, but not burn, and let them stand uncovered till the moisture shall have evaporated. They will then be mealy and in perfection.

ANOTHER.

Pare, wash, and throw them into a pan of cold water; then put them on to boil in a clean pot with cold water sufficient to cover them, and sprinkle over a little salt; then let them boil slowly, uncovered, till you can pass a fork through them; pour off the water, and put them where they will keep hot till wanted. When done in this way, they will be very mealy and dry. Potatoes, either boiled or roasted, should never be covered to keep them hot.

ANOTHER.

Let the potatoes be of a size; do not put them in the pot until the water boils. When done, pour off the water, and remove the cover, until all the steam is gone. Then scatter in half a tea-cupful of suit, and cover the pot with a towel. By adopting this plan, watery potatoes will be mealy. The above receipt is a very important one; but few know how to boil potatoes, and but few of those who know, practice it.

80. VEGETABLE SOUP.

Take a shin of beef, six large carrots, six large yellow onions, twelve turnips, one pound of rice or barley, parsley, leeks, summer savory; put all into a soup kettle, and let it boil four hours; add pepper and salt to taste; serve altogether. It makes a good family soup.

81. BRILLA SOUP.

Take a shin of beef, cut off all the meat in square pieces, then boil the bone three hours; strain it and take off the fat, then put the broth to boil with the pieces of meat, a few carrots and turnips cut small, and a good sprig of thyme, some onions chopped, and a stick of celery cut in pieces; stir them all till the meat is tender. If not cooking brown, you must color it.

82 SOUP.

Take care of the liquor in which poultry and meat has been boiled, as an addition of peas, herbs, &c., will convert it into a nourishing soup.

83. TO DRESS CELERY.

Beat up well one yolk of egg; add two table spoonfuls of cream, one of white sugar, three of vinegar, a teaspoonful of olive oil, one of made mustard, and a pinch of salt. Cut the celery into bits, and add the rest.

VEGETABLES.

84. DRYING PUMPKINS.

Take the ripe pumpkins, pare, cut into small pieces, stew soft, mash and strain through a cullender, as if for making pies. Spread this pulp on plates in layers not quite an inch thick; dry it down in the stove oven, kept at so low a temperature as not to scorch it. In about a day it will become dry and crisp. The sheets thus made can be stowed away in a dry place, and they are always ready for use for pies or sauce. Soak the pieces over night in a little milk, and they will return to a nice pulp, as delicious as the fresh pumpkin,—we think much more so. The quick drying, after cooking, prevents any portion from slightly souring, as is always the case when the uncooked pieces are dried.

Squashes may be prepared in the same way.

85. GREEN PEAS.

Green peas should be young and fresh shelled; wash them clean; put them into a bag, and that into a plenty of boiling water, with a little salt, and a tea-spoonful of pounded loaf sugar; boil them until tender. Green peas are a most delicoius vegetable when cooked enough; half done, they are hard and very unwholesome. It takes from half an hour to an hour to boil them. Never let them stand in the water after they are done. Season them with a little butter and salt.

86. ONIONS.

It is a good plan to boil onions in milk and water; it diminishes the strong taste of that vegetable. It is an excellent way of serving up onions to chop them after they are boiled, and put them into a stew-pan with little milk, butter, salt and pepper, and let them stew about fifteen minutes. This gives them a fine flavor.

87. TO COOK TOMATOES.

Peel and put them into a stew-pan, with a table-spoonful of water, if not very juicy; if so, no water will be required. Put in a little salt, and stew them for half an hour; then turn them into a deep dish with buttered toast. Another way of cooking them, which is considered very nice by epicures, is to put them into a deep dish, with fine bread crumbs, crackers pounded fine, a layer of each alternately; put small bits of butter, a little salt and pepper on each layer; some cooks add a little nutmeg and sugar. Have a layer of bread crumbs on the top. Bake it three-quarters of an hour.

88. GREEN BEANS.

String beans take nearly an hour and a half to boil. Shell beans from an hour to an hour and a quarter. Put them on in boiling water.

89. SWEET CORN.

It is much sweeter when boiled in the cob. If made into sucatash, cut it from the cobs, and boil it with Lima or Sibby beans, and a few slices of salt pork. It requires boiling from fifteen to thirty minutes, according to its age.

90. BAKED BEANS AND PEAS.

Soak them several hours, then put them over the fire in fresh water, let them cook slowly, if you wish to bake them so they will not break to pieces. Change the water two or three times. Salt them and bake in a deep pan. The water should cover them at least an inch when placed in the oven.

91. CORN OYSTERS.

Grate young sweet corn into a dish, and to a pint add one egg well beaten, a small tea-cup of flour, half a gill of cream, and a tea-spoonful of salt. Mix it well together. Fry it exactly like oysters, dropping it into the fat by spoonfuls, about the size of an oyster.

BREAD AND BISCUIT.

92. WHITE BREAD.

Mix in six pounds of sifted flour, one ounce of salt, half a pint of fresh, sweet yeast, and a sufficient quantity of warm milk to make the whole into a stiff dough; work and knead it well on a board upon which a little flour has been sprinkled, for ten or fifteen minutes, then put it in a deep pan, cover it with a warm towel, set it before the fire, and let it rise an hour and a half, or two hours, then knead it well and bake.

93. INDIAN LOAF BREAD.

Stir Indian meal in skim milk to the consistency of pancake butter, about two quarts. Add two table-spoonfuls of molasses, one of saleratus, two of shortening, and two teacupfuls of wheat flour. Stir in the evening, bake in the morning, and eat while hot.

94. RYE AND INDIAN BREAD.

Take four quarts of sifted Indian meal; put into a glazed earthen pan, sprinkle over it a table-spoonful of fine salt, pour over it about two quarts of boiling water, stir and work it till every part of the meal is thoroughly wet; when it is about milk-warm, work in two quarts of rye meal, half a pint of lively yeast, mixed with a pint of warm water; add more warm water if needed. Work the mixture well with your hands; it should be stiff, but not as firm as flour dough. Have ready a large, deep, well buttered pan; put in the dough. Set this to rise in a warm place in the winter; in the summer it should not be put by the fire. When it begins to crack on the top, which will usually be in about an hour or an hour **and a half, put it** into a well heated oven, and bake it three or **four hours.** It is **better to** let it stand in the **oven all** night, unless **the weather is warm. Indian** meal requires to be well cooked. **The loaf will weigh** between seven and eight pounds.

95. GOOD BROWN BREAD.

Take one **quart of** Indian meal, and **three pints of rye** meal; put into a pan, turn about **half a cupfull of molasses,** and two tea-spoonfuls of ginger into **it. Take** some saleratus, dissolve in warm water, enough to mix the meal rather soft; let it remain in the pan to rise over night. When light enough, put it in pans and bake it. Bread made so, will not sour so quick as when yeast is put into it.

96. BROWN OR DYSPEPSIA BREAD.

This bread is now best known as the "Graham Bread," not that Dr. Graham invented or discovered the manner of its preparation, but that he has **been** unwearied and successful in recommending it to the public. **It** is an excellent article of diet for the dyspeptic **and the** costive; and for most persons of sedentary habits it would be beneficial. It agrees well with **children; and, in short, I** think it should be used in every family, though not to the exclusion of fine **bread.** The most difficult point in manufacturing this bread **is to** obtain good pure **meal. It is** said that much of the **bread** commonly sold **as** dyspepsia, **is made of the bran or** middlings, **from** which the fine flour has been **separated**; and that *saw-dust* is sometimes **mixed with the meal.** To be certain that it is good, send good clean wheat to the mill, have it ground rather coarsely, and keep the meal in a dry, cool place. Before using it, sift it through a common hair-sieve; this will separate the very coarse and hard particles.

Take six **quarts of the wheat** meal, **one** tea-cupfull of good yeast, and half a tea-cup of molasses; mix these with a pint of milk-warm water, and a tea-spoonful of pearlash or saleratus. Make a hole in the flour, and stir this mixture in the middle of the meal till it is like batter. Then proceed as with fine flour bread. Make the dough, when sufficiently light, into four loaves, which will weigh two pounds per loaf when baked. It requires a hotter oven than fine flour bread, and must bake about an hour and a half.

97. RYE AND INDIAN BREAD.

There are many different proportions of mixing it; some put one-third of Indian meal and two of rye; others like one-third rye, and two of Indian; others prefer it half and half. If you use the largest proportion of rye meal, make your dough stiff so that it will mould into loaves; when it is two-thirds Indian, it should be softer, and baked in deep earthen or tin pans, after the following manner:

Take four quarts of sifted Indian meal, put it into a glazed earthen pan. Sprinkle over it a table-spoonful of fine salt, pour over it about two quarts of boiling water. Stir and work it till every part of the meal is thoroughly wet. Indian absorbs a greater quantity of water. When it is about milk-warm, work in two quarts of rye meal, half a pint of lively yeast, mixed with a pint of warm water; add more water if needed. Work the mixture well with your hands; it should be stiff, but not so firm as flour dough. Have ready a large, deep, well buttered pan; put in the dough, and smooth the top by putting your hand in warm water and then patting down the loaf. Set this to rise in a warm place in the winter; in the summer it should not be put by the fire. When it begins to crack on the top, which will usually be in about an hour, put it into a well-heated oven, and bake it three or four hours. It is better to let it stand in the oven all night, unless the weather is warm. Indian meal requires to be well cooked; the loaf will weigh between seven and eight pounds. Pan bread keeps best in large loaves.

Many use milk in mixing bread. In the country, where the milk is plentiful, it is a good practice, as bread is certainly sweeter wet with sweet milk than with water; but it will not keep so long in warm weather. Baking can very well be done in a stove; during the winter, this is an economical way of cooking; but the stove must be carefully watched, or their is danger of scorching the bread.

98. BROWN BREAD.

Six quarts of Indian meal, one of rye, sift into the Indian; two table-spoonfuls of molasses, mix with warm water, one table-spoonful of saleratus, and a little salt.

A very nice loaf of brown bread may also be made in the following manner, and it will seldom trouble the most delicate stomach:— One and a half pints of Indian meal, one and a half pints of Graham or coarse wheat meal, one and a half pints of sour milk, two small teaspoons of soda, three spoons molasses, and one teaspoon of salt. Dissolve the soda in about half a pint of hot water, and mix all together. Bake two or three hours in a slow oven. This loaf is very nice to be steamed in a deep pot, with a tight cover, three or four hours. Put your bread in a tin pail with a close cover, and don't let the water get into the pail.

99. DYSPEPSIA BREAD.

Take three quarts of unbolted wheat meal, one quart soft warm water, one gill of fresh yeast, one gill of molasses, and one tea-spoonful of saleratus.

100. PUMPKIN BREAD.

Take a pumpkin, pare it, cut it up, then boil in water till it becomes quite thick; add flour so as to make it dough.

101. SAGO BREAD.

One pound of sago, well soaked in water or milk several hours, mix it with as much flour, add saleratus, good yeast, and a little Indian meal if liked. Let it rise, and then bake.

102. RYE AND INDIAN BREAD.

Mix two quarts of each with three pints of boiling milk, table-spoon salt, and stir well. Let it stand till lukewarm, then stir in half a pint of good yeast. Knead to a stiff dough, and put to rise near the fire. When the top is cracked over, make into two loaves, and bake moderate two and a half hours.

103. CHEAP BREAD.

Indian meal is the cheapest, and a bushel furnishes more

nutriment than the same quantity of wheat. It is also a generally healthy diet, and those who wish to practice close economy, should use much of this meal in their families.

104. CORN MEAL BREAD AND CAKE.

It is astonishing how many ways, and at what a cheap rate corn meal can be cooked, to make nice, nutritious, and healthful bread and cake for the human family. At an exhibition of corn meal and cake, held by Mr. Orange Judd, the editor and proprietor of the American Agriculturist, three premiums of ten, five, and two dollars each were awarded for corn bread, and four and two dollars each for corn cake. There were over two hundred samples for the committee to decide upon. We give the recipes of the successful ones, in the order in which they received their premiums, for the benefit of our readers:—

Take two quarts of corn meal, with about a pint of (thin) bread sponge, and water enough to wet it. Mix in one half pint of wheat flour, and a table spoonful of salt. Let it rise and knead well the second time. Bake one and a half hours.

The following took the second prize:— Mix two quarts of new corn meal with three pints of warm water. Add one table-spoonful of salt, two table-spoonfuls of sugar, and one large table-spoonful of hop yeast. Let it stand in a warm place five hours to rise. Then add three-fourths of a pint of wheat flour, and one-half a pint of warm water. Let it rise again one and a half hours; then pour it into a pan well greased with sweet lard, and let it rise a few minutes. Then bake in a moderately hot oven one and a half hours. It is best when hot.

The following was awarded to the third premium:—Take two quarts of white corn meal, one table-spoonful of lard, and one pint of hot water. Mix the lard in water, stir it well that it may get heated thoroughly, and add one-half pint of cold water. When the mixture is cool enough, add two well-beaten eggs, and two table-spoonsful of home made yeast. Bake one hour in a moderate heated oven. If for breakfast, make over night.

The following received the first premium for corn meal

cake:— Take three tea-cupfuls of corn meal, one tea-cupful of wheat flour, two table-spoonfuls of brown sugar, two tea-spoonfuls of cream of tartar, and one tea-spoonful of **salt**. Mix well together *while dry*. Add one tea-spoonful of soda, (or saleratus,) dissolved in warm water. Mix the whole to a thin batter, and bake in a quick oven three-quarters of an hour. The same batter will bake quicker in patty cans, or on a griddle, like buckwheat cakes.

To the following was awarded the second premium:— **Take eight eggs, and their** weight in powdered sugar; the **weight of six eggs of Indian** meal, one-half pound of butter, and one nutmeg. Beat the whites and the yolks of the eggs separately; adding the whites last; bake one hour.

We also copy from the same paper other recipes for cooking corn meal, furnished by contributors to that journal.

Take **two** quarts **of** Indian meal, **one pint** of sifted wheat **bran,** one-half tea-cupful of molasses, one-half tea-spoonful each of salt and **cooking** soda, or saleratus. Mix with sweet milk enough to make a batter as stiff as can be readily stirred with an iron spoon. Bake six hours.

Take **four** to six quarts of Indian **meal, and scald** two-thirds of it, stirring thoroughly **with an iron spoon**; cool with cold water until it will not cook the yeast, and add one **pint** of good salt yeast. Stir in the remainder of the meal, **put it in a pan to rise, the** same as **light** wheat **bread, and afterwards bake it** well, and **keep it in a cool, dry place. Good** when one to four days old.

105. RICE BREAD.

One quart of rice meal, one pint of milk, one table-spoonful of butter, **two** eggs, one table-spoonful of tartaric **acid,** dissolved in a wine-glass of water, one tea-spoonful of soda dissolved in **a wine-glass of water**; put the acid in **first.** Bake immediately.

RICE BREAD.

Take one pound and a half of rice, **and boil it** gently over a slow fire, in three quarts of water, about five hours, stirring it, and afterwards beating it up in a smooth paste. Mix this, while warm, in two gallons, or four pounds of flour, adding at the same time the usual quantity of yeast. Allow the dough to work a certain time near the fire, after which divide it into loaves, and it will be found, when baked, to produce **twenty-eight or thirty pounds of good white bread.**

106. SCOTCH BREAD.

One **pound and a quarter** of flour, three-quarters of sugar, and three-quarters of butter; essence of lemon to taste. Bake twenty minutes in rather a slow oven.

107. RYE-MEAL BREAD.

Two quarts of rye-meal, one of flour, three-quarters cup of molasses, three-quarters cup of yeast. Add enough warm water to make a quart; a little salt.

108. PREMIUM WHEAT AND INDIAN BREAD.

One quart of new milk, one tea-cup of home made hop yeast, one tea-spoon of salt, and one-half pound of Indian meal; boil the milk, scald the meal; when cool enough, add flour and yeast enough for a sponge. When risen light, add flour sufficient enough for smooth loaf; let it rise again before putting in pans.

109. RICE BREAD AND MUFFINS.

One cup of rice, before boiled, one quart of milk, half cup of sugar, small piece of butter, stir in flour enough to make a thick batter, a cup of yeast; boil the rice very soft. It is very good, made of a pint of milk, and no sugar.

110. MILK BISCUIT.

Take two quarts of flour, one pint of sour milk, one-half cup full of lard or butter, two tea-spoonsful of saleratus' one of salt; knead the whole together and bake quick.

111. SODA BISCUIT.

Take two quarts of flour, four tea-spoonfuls of cream tartar, one of salt, two of saleratus or soda, and a small piece of butter for shortening; mix with water.

112. BISCUIT OR ROLLS.

Put two tea-spoonfuls of cream tartar finely pulverized, into one quart of dry flour, then dissolve three-fourths of a tea-spoonful of sup. carb. of soda in warm new milk, sufficient when mingled with the flour, to make the paste of the ordinary consistence of soft biscuit; then mix and bake in forms of rolls or biscuit, for about twenty minutes.

113. ARROWROOT DROPS, OR BISCUITS.

Half a pound of butter, beaten up to a cream, seven eggs well whisked, adding seven ounces of flour, six ounces of arrowroot, and half a pound of loaf sugar; mix well together, and drop on a clean tin, size of a shilling; bake in a slow oven.

114. BLOCK BISCUITS.

Half a pound of butter beaten up to a cream, half a pound of ground rice, three-quarters of a pound of flour, half a pound of loaf sugar, four eggs, and a little saleratus.

115. CINNAMON BISCUIT.

Half a pound of dry flour, one pound of lump sugar, finely sifted, one pound of butter, sixpennyworth of powdered cinnamon. The whole to be mixed with a glass of brandy, then rolled very thin, and baked in a quick oven.

116. RECEIPTS FOR MAKING YEAST.

Boil, say on Monday, two ounces of the best hops in four quarts of water, for half an hour; strain it, and let the liquid cool down to new milk warm, then put in a handful of salt and a half pound of sugar; beat up one pound of the best of flour with some of the liquor, and then mix well together. On Wednesday, add three pounds of potatoes, boiled and then mashed. Let them stand together till Thursday; then strain, put it into bottles, and it is ready for use.

It must be stirred frequently while it is making, and kept near the fire. Before using, shake the bottle up well. It will keep in a cool place two months, and is best the latter part of the time. It ferments spontaneously, not requiring the aid of other yeast, and if care be taken to let it ferment well in the earthen bowl in which it is made, you may cork it up tight when bottled.

HOME-MADE YEAST.

Take a handful of loose hops, (a pinch only of pressed ones,) and tie in a bit of muslin; boil twenty minutes, in two quarts of water; take them out and throw in four sliced potatoes, and boil till soft; strain all through a sieve, and add half a tea-cup of salt, and the same of brown sugar; scald these, and let it stand till luke-warm; add sufficient yeast to rise it. When quite light, or when it ceases to bubble up, put it in a jug or covered jar, set it in a cool place, and it will keep good a fortnight in hot weather, or a month in cold.

YEAST.

In summer bread should be mixed with cold water. In damp weather the water should be tepid, and in cold weather quite warm. If the yeast is new, a small quantity will make the bread rise. In the country, yeast cakes are found very convenient, but they seldom make the bread as good as fresh lively yeast. The following is a good receipt:— Boil for half an hour two quarts of water thickened with about three spoonfuls of wheat flour, and sweetened with two tea-cups of molasses. When nearly cold, put it into a jug, adding four spoonfuls of fresh yeast. Shake it well, and place it uncovered near the fire for one day to ferment. There will be a thin liquor on top, pour this off, shake the remainder, and cork it up for use. Yeast will not generally keep good over ten days.

POTATO YEAST.

Boil potatoes soft, boil and mash them, and add as much water as will make them the consistency of common yeast; while the potatoes are warm, put in half a tea-cupful of molasses, and two table-spoonfuls of yeast. Let it stand near the fire until done fermenting, when it will be fit for use.

HOP YEAST.

In two quarts of water, boil a handful of hops; strain and pour the liquor hot upon half a tea-cup of wheat-flour. When about milk warm, add a tea-cupful of yeast. Let it ferment, when it will be ready for use, and it may be bottled.

TO MAKE GOOD YEAST.

Take as many hops as you can hold in your hands twice; put them into three pints of cold water; put them over the fire, and let them boil twenty minutes; then strain the water in an earthen or stone jar, and stir in, while the water is scalding hot, flour enough to make a stiff batter; let it stand till about milk-warm; then add a tea-cupful of old yeast to make it rise, and a tea-spoonful of saleratus dissolved in the old yeast; stir it well, and put the jar in a warm place to rise. Some add Indian meal enough (after it has risen well) to make into cakes and dry it on a board in the sun. This is very convenient, especially in hot weather; a small cake soaked in warm water, is enough to make a large pan of dough rise.

YEAST.

Boil one pound of flour, a quarter of a pound of brown sugar, and a little salt, in two gallons of water, for an hour. When milk-warm, bottle and cork it close, and it will be ready for use in twenty-four hours.

PRESERVES AND JELLIES.

Preserves of all kinds should be kept entirely secluded from the air, and in a dry place. In ranging them on the shelves of a store-closet, they should not be suffered to come in contact with the wall. Moisture, in winter and spring, exudes from some of the dryest walls, and preserves invariably imbibe it, both in dampness and taste. It is necessary, occasionally to look at them, and if they have been attacked by mould, boil them up gently again. To prevent all risks, it is always well to lay a brandy paper over the fruit before tying down. This may be renewed in the spring.

Fruit jellies are made in the ratio of a quart of fruit to two pounds of sugar. They must not be boiled quick, nor very long. Practice, and a general discretion, will be found the best guides to regulate the exact time, which necessarily must be affected, more or less, by local causes.

117. TO PRESERVE BARBERRIES.

To one pound of berries, add one pound of sugar, a pint and a half of molasses, and simmer them together for an hour or more, until they become soft.

118. RASPBERRY JAM.

With equal proportions of pounded loaf (or lump) sugar, and raspberries; put the fruit in a preserving pan, and with a silver spoon, or flat wooden stick, bruise and mash it well. Let it boil up; then add the sugar, stirring it well with the fruit; when it boils, skim it, and then boil it fifteen or twenty minutes.

RASPBERRY JAM.

To one pound of fruit put one pound of sugar; bruise them together in your preserving pan with a spoon, and let them simmer gently for an hour. When cold, put them into glass jars, lay over them a bit of paper saturated with brandy. Tie them up so as to exclude the air.

119. PEACH JAM.

Let your peaches be quite ripe; pare and cut them into small pieces. To every pound of fruit, add one pound of sugar. Put the fruit and sugar into a preserving kettle, mash all together, place it over the fire, and when it begins to cook, stir it until it becomes quite thick. Then take it from the fire, put in glasses, and when cold, tie closely.

129. TO PRESERVE DAMSONS.

To every pound of damsons, allow three-quarters of a pound of powdered sugar; put into jars, or well-glazed earthen pots, alternately a layer of damsons and one of sugar; tie strong paper or cloth over the pots, and set them in the oven after the bread is drawn, and let them stand till the oven is cold. The next day, strain off the syrup, and boil it till thick; when it is cold, put the damsons into small jars or glasses, pour over the syrup, which should cover them, and tie a wet bladder or strong cloth over them.

THE TOMATO AS FOOD.

Dr. Bennett, a professor of some celebrity, considers the tomato an invaluable article of diet, and inscribes to it very important properties :—

1. That the tomato is one of the most powerful asperients of the liver and other organs; where calomel is indicated, it is probably one of the most effective and least harmful remedial agents known to the profession.

2. That a chemical extract will be obtained from it that will supercede the use of calomel in the cure of disease.

3. That he has successfully treated diarrhœa with this article alone.

4. That when used as an article of diet, it is **almost a sovereign** remedy for dyspepsia and indigestion.

5. That it should be constantly used for daily food; either cooked, raw, or in any form of catsup, is the most healthy article now in use.

121. TOMATO CATSUP.

One-half bushel of tomatoes, break them in pieces; put a layer of tomatoes, then a layer of salt; let them stand over night; one-quarter pound of cassia, one-half a pound of cinnamon, two ounces cloves, one gill of white mustard seed, one tea-spoonful (level) of cayenne pepper, two roots horseradish, six good sized onions; mix, and boil until quite dry, then sift it, and add one pint of cider vinegar.

122. TOMATO SAUCE.

One peck of green tomatoes, cut in thin slices, one pint of salt; let them stand twenty-four hours; drain them well, slice six small onions, one-quarter pound of white mustard seed, one ounce cloves, one ounce ground pepper, one ounce allspice; put together in the kettle, and cover with vinegar; stew until clear; when cold, add one cup of sweet oil.

123. TOMATO FIGS.

Take six pounds of sugar, to one peck (or sixteen pounds) of fruit. Scald and remove the skin of the fruit in the usual way. Cook them over a fire, their own juice being sufficient without the addition of water, until the sugar penetrates, and they are clarified. They are then taken out, spread on dishes, flattened and dried in the sun. A small quantity of the syrup should be occasionally sprinkled over them whilst drying; after which, pack them down in boxes, treating each layer with powdered sugar. The syrup is afterwards concentrated and bottled for use. They keep well from year to year, and retain surprisingly their favor, which is nearly that of the best quality of fresh figs. The pear-shaped, or single tomatoes answers the purpose best. Ordinary brown sugar may be used, a large portion of which is retained in the syrup.

124. TO BOIL PEARS.

Pare them only, and put them in a preserving kettle; throw sugar over them, and cover them with boiling water, then boil until tender.

125. TO STEW PEARS.

Pare and quarter them, and fill an earthen jar; pour over a little water, sugar as you choose, and bake a long time.

126. PRESERVED PEARS.

Pare and quarter; to every pound of fruit add one and a half lemons; these to boil in just water enough to cover them till they are soft; put a layer of pears, sugar and lemon, let stand two or three days, pour off the liquor, let it come to a boil; pour it over the fruit in a jar. This is all the cooking that is required.

127. TO PRESERVE GRAPES.

The French preserve grapes the year round, by coating the clusters with lime. The bunches are picked just before they are thoroughly ripe, and dipped in lime water the consistency of thin cream. They are then hung on wires, and when dry are dipped the second time, and then hung up to remain. The lime coating keeps out air, and checks any tendency to decay. When wanted for the table, dip the clusters in warm water to remove the lime.

128. STRAWBERRY JAM.

Pick twelve pounds of very red ripe strawberries, which put into a preserving pan with ten pounds of sugar; place over a sharp fire, keep constantly stirring, boiling it until the surface is covered with clearish bubbles; then try a little upon a cover, and if it sets, fill your jars, cover them with paper, and tie down until wanted.

129. TO PRESERVE QUINCES.

Quinces, if very ripe, are best preserved in the following manner. Pare and cut them in slices an inch thick; take out the cores carefully, so as to have the slices in the form of a ring. Allow a pound of nice white sugar for each pound of the fruit; dissolve it in cold water, having a quart of the latter to a pound of sugar, then put in the sliced quinces, and let them soak in it ten or twelve hours. Put them in a **preserving kettle, and put it on** a moderate fire; cover them over, and let the quinces boil gently; there should be more than enough syrup to cover the quinces. When a broom splinter will go through them easily, take them from the fire and turn them out. In the course of a week, turn the syrup from them, and boil it down, so that there will be just enough to cover the fruit.

130. TO PRESERVE, PEACHES, PLUMS, &c.

September is the best month for peaches, as they are then harder and larger. Weigh the peaches, turn them into a preserving pan full of cold water, with a slice or two of lemon; set them on a slow fire, having ready a sieve and a napkin, and be careful and not do them too much.

Some of the peaches will be ready sooner than others; when they begin to be soft they are done enough; take them out as they become soft, and drain them on a sieve, and let them stand until cold; then make a syrup, to every pound of peaches allowing a pound of sugar; use some of the water in which the peaches were boiled, for the syrup. Crack the pits of half a dozen peaches, throw them into hot water, and remove their skins, then boil them with the syrup you are making. Put the peaches into jars and glasses, and pour the syrup over them.

Cut several round pieces of paper, dip them into brandy, lay them over the preserves and tie up the jars.

This way of preserving peaches, is much preferable to cutting them up and preserving them. The fruit should not be permitted to boil until it becomes shrivelled.

Apricots, Nectarines and Plums, may be preserved in the same manner.

131. RED COLORING FOR JELLY, &c.

Calves-foot jelly may be colored a beautiful crimson-red, by tying up some chips of alkanet-root in a thin muslin bag, and boiling it with the other ingredients. Alkanet is to be bought at any of the druggists, the cost is very trifling, and it has no peculiar taste, and no unwholesome properties.

Before using it, pick it clean, and wash the chips from dust or powder. The more alkanet used, the deeper will be the color. Let it **remain in** the strainer while the jelly is dripping.

132. SCOTCH MARMALADE.

Take a bowl or dish of fresh honey, and before you send it to table, mix with it a sufficiency of orange juice, (passed through a strainer,) to give to it a fine flavor of oranges. Mix the honey and orange juice together. It will be found delicious.

133. HONEY BUTTER.

Good butter eight pounds, and one pound clarified honey. Beat well together. A delicacy for children or sick persons. It generally proves mildly laxative.

134. APPLE BUTTER.

Boil down one barrel of new cider to half a barrel. Have ready a bushel and a half of sweet apples, pared, quartered, and the cores removed; put these to the cider, and let the boiling be continued, stirring the whole constantly, that it may not adhere to the sides of the vessel and burn. When the apples have amalgamated with the cider, and the mass becomes as thick as hasty-pudding, put in powdered allspice. It is now done. It will keep sweet for many years, and is a capital article for the table.

135. CURRANT JELLY.

Pick fine red, but long ripe currants from the stems, bruise them, and strain the juice from a quart at a time, through a thin muslin; wring it gently to get all the liquid; put a pound of white sugar to each pound of juice; stir it until it is all dissolved, set it over a gentle fire, let it become hot and boil for fifteen minutes, then try it by putting a teaspoonful into a saucer; when cold, if it is not firm enough, boil it for a few minutes longer. Or, pick the fruit from the stems, weigh it, and put it into a stone pot; set it in a kettle of hot water, reaching nearly to the top; let it boil till the fruit is hot through, then crush them, and strain the juice from them; put a pound of white sugar to each pint of it, put it over the fire and boil for fifteen minutes; try some in a saucer; when the jelly is thick enough, strain it into small white jars, or glass tumblers; when cold, cover with tissue paper as directed. Glass should be tempered by keeping it in warm water for a short time before pouring any hot liquid in it, otherwise it will crack.

ANOTHER.

Put your currants in a deep pan, mash them thoroughly, and strain the juice through a fine sieve. To every pint of juice allow one pound of the best loaf sugar. Put the juice and sugar in a preserving kettle. Have some isinglass dissolved in warm water, add it to the sugar and juice while cold. Place it over the fire, and let it boil till it jellies. Skim it while it is boiling, and put in glasses while warm. When cold, cover with brandy paper.

Currant jelly is a necessary appendage to all wild meats, and likewise to roast mutton.

136. RHUBARB JAM.

To seven pounds of rhubarb, add four sweet oranges and five pounds of sugar. Peel and cut up the rhubarb. Put in the thin peel of the oranges and the pulp, after taking out the seeds and all the whites. Boil all together for one hour and a half.

137. APPLE SAUCE.

Pare, core, and slice some apples, and put them in a stone jar, into a saucepon of water, or on a hot hearth. If on a hearth, let a spoonful or two of water be put in to keep them from burning. When they are done, bruise them to a mash, and put to them a piece of butter the size of a nutmeg, and a little brown sugar if required; but it destroys the slight acid flavor of the apples, and its corrective to goose and pork.

138. APPLE ISLAND.

Stew apples enough to make a quart, strain it through a

sieve, sweeten with fine white sugar, and flavor it with lemon or rose. Beat the whites of six eggs to a hard froth, and stir into the apple slowly, but do not do this until just before it is to be served. The apple should be stewed with as little water as possible. Put it into a glass dish. Serve **a nice,** boiled custard, made of the yolks of the eggs, to eat **with it.**

139. ORANGE MARMALADE.

One pound of oranges, half a pound of lemons, three quarts of water. Boil slowly for two hours; cut all, taking out the seeds. To each pound of fruit take two pounds of loaf sugar, and one pint of the water in which the fruit was boiled. While cutting the fruit into thin slices, pour the **water** upon the sugar, and **then boil all together** for half an hour.

140. APPLE JELLY.

Take as many apples as you would like amount of jelly, say a brass kettle full; cut them without paring or coreing, and boil till soft; then put them into a bag and drain the liquor off, which boil down half; then add the weight of it in sugar; boil together fifteen minutes, or till the jelly comes; pour in moulds

141. TO BAKE APPLES.

Take sour apples, those of a keen **acid, and to every** square **tin filled** with them, pour over a tea-cupful **of** sugar. Bake them slowly until done. Eat them with cream, and the juice that cooks from them. No one knows much about baked apples, who has not eaten them in this way. No quince, **pear,** peach **or** plum preserves, equal this simple dessert.

ANOTHER.

Select **the largest** apples, scoop **out the** core without cutting quite through; fill the hollow with butter and fine soft sugar. Let them roast in a slow oven, and serve up with the syrup.

142. POACHED EGGS.

Break the eggs into a pan; beat them to a froth; then put them into a buttered tin pan; set the pan on to a few coals; put in a small lump of butter and a little salt; let them cook very slowly, stirring them constantly, till they become quite thick; then turn them on to buttered toast.

143. TO BOIL EGGS.

To try the freshness of eggs, put them into a pan of cold water; those that sink are the best. Always let the water boil before putting the eggs in. Three minutes will boil them soft; four minutes the whites will be completely done, and in six minutes they will be sufficiently hard for garnishings salads and dishes requiring them.

144. EGG OMELETS.

Six eggs, half a cup of milk, a little salt; fry in batter.

145. FRUIT CREAMS.

Half an ounce of isinglass, dissolved in a little water; then put a pint of good cream, sweetened to taste; boil it; when nearly cold, lay some apricot or raspberry jam on the bottom of a glass dish, and pour over; this is most excellent.

146. CHARLOTTE RUSSE.

Take an oval or oblong sponge cake; excavate the middle, leaving the bottom and sides about one-inch thick; line the cake with a thick layer of raspberry, or any kind of jelly. Then prepare a rich boiled custard, and pour it into the cavity; whip the whites of eggs to a stiff froth, and heap upon the top. Set it upon ice till needed.

147. BLANC MANGE.

To one ounce of isinglass, put a pint of water; boil it till the isinglass is melted, with a bit of cinnamon; put it to three-quarters of a pint of cream, and a bit of lemon peel; sweeten it; stir it over the fire: let it boil, strain, and let it cool; squeeze in the juice of a lemon, and put into moulds.

BLANC MANGE MADE WITH MOSS.

Wash the moss in many waters, carefully draining it, till every particle of saline taste is removed. Take one quart of milk, add a handful of the moss, and set it over the fire. Let it come to a boil gently, and simmer fifteen minutes. Strain it into a dish, and flavor with lemon. It may be poured into moulds.

ARROW ROOT BLANC MANGE.

Boil one quart of milk, salt it, add four table spoonfuls of sugar, and stir into it three table-spoonfuls of arrow root, dissolved in a little water. Let it boil five minutes and flavor to your taste.

148. BRANDY PEACHES.

To one pound of peaches add one pound of sugar; pick the peaches, turn hot water over them, adding a little saleratus; make a syrup of one quart of water, eight pounds sugar; boil the peaches ten or fifteen minutes; when cold, add one pint of syrup one pint of brandy.

149 CUP CUSTARDS.

One quart of cream, or new milk, nutmeg, eight eggs, one ounce of sugar. Boil the eggs and sugar well together, grate in some nutmeg, add the cream by degrees, stirring it all the while; set your custard cups in a dripping-pan, pour the custard into the cups, set the dripping pan into the oven, then pour water around. Bake in a quick oven.

150. ORANGE CUSTARDS.

One Seville orange, one-half ounce of loaf sugar, four eggs, rose water, one pint of cream. Squeeze the juice from a Seville orange, take half of the peel and boil very tender, beat in a (marble) mortar, until fine; put to it two spoons of rose water, the juice of the orange, the sugar and the yellows of the eggs. Beat all together for ten minutes, then have ready the cream boiling hot, which put to them by degrees; beat them until cold, then put them into custard cups, in a dish of hot water. Let them stand until they are set, then take them out and stick preserved orange peel on the top. This forms a fine flavored dish, and may be served up hot or cold.

151. ICE CURRANTS.

Take large bunches of red currants, have them clean, whisk the white of an egg to a froth, and dip them in it, lay them on a sieve or plate, not to be touched, sift double refined sugar over them, very thick, and dry them in a cool oven.

152. ICING FOR CAKE.

Two pounds of double refined sugar, one spoon of fine starch, one pennyworth gum Arabic in powder, five eggs, one spoon rose-water, one juice of lemon. Make the sugar fine, and sift it through a hair sieve, rub the starch fine, sift, and the gum Arabic sift also; beat or stir all well together. Take the whites of the eggs, whisk them well, put one spoonful of rose water, one spoon of the juice of lemon, beat well together, then put to the sugar by degrees, until you wet it, then beat it until the cake is baked; lay it on with a knife, and the ornaments, if you have any; if it does not harden sufficiently from the warmth of the cake, return it to the oven. Be careful not to discolor.

153. ICE CREAM.

Two quarts of milk, twelve eggs, two ounces of sugar, two lemons. Grate the peels into the milk, and boil; sweeten; take the yellows of all the eggs, and half of the whites; beat them well, then add the boiling milk, keep them stirring, set the dish over the fire for five minutes, stirring it constantly; then pour through a sieve into your freezing-pot. The proportions to surround the pot, is one quart of salt, to one pail full of ice. Place it in as cold a place as possible; as fast as it freezes on the sides, remove it with a spoon. One hour is sufficient to freeze it.

ICE CREAM.

Any preserved fruit, five pounds; cream, one gallon; juice of six lemons, sugar to sweeten. Pass the whole through a sieve, then put it into the freezing-pot, and work it until frozen.

154. ICE CREAM WITH FRUIT.

One pound of preserved fruit, one quart of cream, two lemons, cochineal. **Squeeze** the juice of the lemons into some sugar to taste; **then** pass all through a sieve, and if raspberry, **or** strawberry, or **any** other ripe fruit, **add** a little cochineal to heighten the color. Have the freezing-pot nice and clear, put the cream into it **and** cover it; then put the pot **into** the tub with the **ice** beat small, and some salt; turn **the freezing** pot quick, and **as** the cream sticks to the sides, **scrape it down** with **an** ice-spoon, and **so** on until it is frozen. The more the **cream is worked to the side** with a spoon, the smoother and better it will be flavored. After it is well frozen, take it out, **and** put it into ice shapes with salt and ice; then carefully wash the shapes for fear of any salt adhering to **them**; dip them into lukewarm water, and **send** to the table. Fresh fruit, strawberries or raspberries, are nice, **but more** sugar will be necessary.

155. SNOW CREAM.

Beat the whites of four eggs to a froth, and stir in two spoonsful of white sugar; flavor with rose water or lemon; add a pint of thick, sweet cream, and beat the whole together to a froth. This is to be served with a dessert of sweetmeats.

156. CREAM CUSTARD.

Mix **a pint** of **cream** with one **of** milk, **five** beaten eggs, **a** table-spoonful of flour and **one of** sugar. Add nutmeg to **the** taste, and bake the custards **in** cups or pie-plates, in a quick oven.

157. CHERRY ICE CREAM.

Pound half a pound of preserved cherries, unstoned; put them into a basin with a pint of cream, the juice of a lemon, and a gill of syrup; pass it through a sieve, and freeze it in the usual way.

158. CURRANT ICE CREAM.

Put into a basin a large table-spoonful and a half of currant jelly, with half **a** gill of syrup; squeeze in the juice of one lemon and a half, and add a pint of cream and a little cochineal; pass it through **a** sieve; freeze in the usual way.

DESSERT AND SIDE DISHES. 63

ICE CREAM.

Two quarts of good rich milk, four fresh eggs, three-quarters of a pound of white sugar, six tea-spoons of Bermuda arrow-root. Rub the arrow-root smooth in a little cold milk, beat the eggs and sugar together, bring the milk to the boiling point, then stir in the arrow root, remove it then from the fire, and immediately add the eggs and sugar, stirring briskly to keep the eggs from cooking, then set aside to cool. If flavored with extracts, let it be done *just before* putting it in the freezer.

159. PINE APPLE CREAM.

Grate the pulp of the fruit, add sugar, mix with the cream and freeze. Peaches, pears, strawberries, and raspberries, may be prepared in the same way, and are very delicious.

160. LOBSTER SALAD.

Select a large lobster; pick out the meat and pull it into shreds with two forks. Boil two eggs six minutes, till hard, and let them cool. Mash them smooth with a knife and spoon, add a spoonful of vinegar, one of salt, one of mustard, and three table spoonsful of salad oil. Stir well, and incorporate the meat of the lobster, till the whole is a solid mass; lastly, mince the lettuce fine, and stir it in just before serving; garnish with sliced boiled egg, lobster claws and parsley.

161. ASPARAGUS AND EGGS.

Toast a slice of bread, butter it, and lay it on a dish; butter some eggs thus:— take four eggs, beat them well, put them in a sauce-pan with two ounces of butter, and a little salt, until of a sufficient consistence, and lay them on the toast. Meanwhile, boil some asparagus tender, cut the ends small, and lay them on the eggs.

162. ASPARAGUS, BOILED.

Scrape and tie them in a small bundle; cut them even, boil them quick in salt and water; lay them on a toast dipped in the water the asparagus was boiled in; pour over them melted butter.

PASTRY—PIES.

163. PIE-CRUST.

To make good pie-crust, use half a pound of shortening **to a pound** of flour. Crust looks nicest made with lard, but it tastes better to have butter used in making it. In winter beef shortening mixed with butter, makes a good plain pie-crust. Use a tea-spoonful of salt to each pound of flour; when the shortening is thoroughly mixed with the flour, add just sufficient cold water to render it moist enough to roll out easily. Pastry should be baked in a quick oven. In cold weather, warm **the shortening before** using it for pie-crust, but it must **not be melted, or the** crust will not be flaky.

164. PLAIN CUSTARD PIE.

Boil a quart **of milk with the rind of a** lemon. When it has flavored **the** milk, **strain it and set** it where it will boil. Mix a table-spoonful **of flour,** smoothly, with a couple of table-spoonsfuls of milk, and stir it into the boiling-milk. Let it boil a minute, stirring it constantly; take it from the fire, and **when cool, put in** three beaten eggs; sweeten it to the taste, **turn it into deep** pie-plates, and bake the pies **directly in a quick oven.**

165. RHUBARB PIES.

Take the tender stock of the rhubarb, strip off the **skin,** and cut the stalks into thin slices. Line deep plates **with** pie-crust, then put in the rhubarb, with a thick layer of sugar to each layer of rhubarb; a little grated lemon peel improves the pie. Cover the pies with a crust, press it down tight round the edge of the plate, and prick the crust with a fork, so that it will not burst while baking, and let out the juices of the pie. Rhubarb pies should be baked about an hour in a slow oven. It will not do to bake them quick.

166. CUSTARD PIES.

Take six beaten eggs to a quart of milk, sweeten with sugar. Do not bake them too much.

167. PUMPKIN PIES.

Pare and stew the pumpkin, then strain it through a coarse sieve. Take two quarts of scalded milk, six eggs, stir the pumpkin into it, sweeten with sugar or molasses. Salt it, and spice with ginger, cinnamon, or grated lemon peel. Bake with a bottom crust. Crackers pounded fine are a good substitute for eggs.

PUMPKIN PIE.

Stew the pumpkin dry, and make it like squash pie; only season rather higher. Part cream with the milk, gives it a richer flavor. Roll the paste rather thicker than for fruit pies, as there is but one crust. Bake about an hour in a brisk oven; if large and deep, bake a little longer.

168. PIGEON PIE.

Border a large dish with fine puff paste, and cover the bottom with a veal cutlet, or tender stake, free from fat and bone, and seasoned with salt, cayenne and nutmeg; prepare with great nicety as many fresh-killed pigeons as the dish will contain in one layer; put into each a slice of butter, seasoned with cayenne; lay them into the dish with the breasts downwards, and between and over them put the yolks of half a dozen of hard boiled eggs; stick plenty of butter on them, season the whole well with salt and spice, pour in some cold water for the gravy, roll out the cover three-quarters of an inch thick, secure it well round the edge, ornament it highly, and bake it for an hour or more in a well heated oven.

169. OYSTER PATTIES.

Line some small patty-pans with a fine puff paste; put a piece of bread into each, cover with paste and bake them. While they are baking, take some oysters and cut them into small pieces; place them in a saucepan with a very small portion of grated nutmeg, a very little white pepper and salt, a morsel of lemon peel, cut as small as possible, a little cream, and a little of the oyster liquor; simmer it a few minutes, then remove the bread from the patties, and put in the mixture.

170. POTATO PIE.

As many potatoes washed and sliced as will fill a pie-dish, a little salt and pepper, a sprinkling of finely chopped onions, a tea-cupful of cream, (or good milk,) a bit of butter the size of a walnut, cover over with a meat pie-crust, and bake till the potatoes are thoroughly done. If crust is not approved, it is good without.

POTATO PIE.

One pound of boiled potatoes, rolled fine, half a pound of butter, six eggs, eight spoonsfuls of milk, the grated peel and juice of a lemon, sugar and salt to your taste. To be baked in deep plates.

171. MINCE PIE.

Boil three pounds of lean beef till tender, and when cold chop it fine. Chop three pounds of clear beef suet, and mix the meat, sprinkling in a tea-spoonful of salt.

Pare, core and chop fine, six pounds of good apples; stone four pounds of raisins and chop them; wash and dry two pounds of currants; and mix them all well with the meat. Season with a spoonful of powdered cinnamon, a powdered nutmeg, a little mace, and a few cloves, pounded, and one pound of brown sugar; add a quart of cider, and half a pound of citron cut into small bits. This mixture, put down in a stone jar, and closely covered, will keep several weeks. It makes a rich pie for Thanksgiving and Christmas.

MINCE PIE.

One cracker and a half, three spoonfuls of melted butter, a cup of vinegar, one cup of molasses, raisins and spices to your taste. Melt the butter and vinegar, then add the rest, and fill your paste. Cover as usual. This, if well made, can hardly be distinguished from a mince pie of meat and apples.

MOCK MINCE PIES.

Three crackers, half a cup of vinegar, one cup of raisins, half a cup of hot water, half a cup of sugar, four spoonsful of molasses, two eggs, a small piece of butter; spice the same as for mince pies.

172. LEMON PIE.

For one pie, take a couple of good sized fresh lemons, squeeze out the juice, and mix it with a half pint of molasses, or sufficient sugar to make the juice sweet. Chop the peel fine, line deep pie plates with your pastry, then sprinkle on a layer of your chopped lemon peel, turn in part of the mixed sugar or molasses and juice, then cover the whole with pie-crust rolled very thin, put in another layer of peel, sweetened juice and crust, and so till all the lemon is used. Cover the whole with a thick crust, and bake the pie about half an hour.

LEMON PIE.

Make a nice paste, and lay into two medium sized plates; then prepare the following mixture:—To the juice of one lemon, made very sweet with white sugar, add three well-beaten eggs, and a piece of butter half the size of an egg, melted. Stir the ingredients together, then add a pint of rich milk or thin cream, stirring very fast. Fill the plates and bake immediately.

LEMON PIE.

Juice of three lemons, peel grated of two; two eggs, two tea-cups of sugar, five table spoons of corn starch. Wet first with cold water, and then with boiling water, to thicken it. Don't have it too thick. Bake like custards. Makes two pies.

LEMON PIE.

Three eggs, separate the yolks from the whites, one cup of sugar, grate the rind of two lemons, extract the juice, keep one spoonful of sugar for the whites of the eggs, for a frosting to the pie; after it is baked, put it back in the oven; slightly brown it.

LEMON PIE.

Grate the rind of two lemons, then squeeze all the juice out, adding the grating to the juice, then add a cup and a half of sugar, and the same of water; four powdered crackers, three eggs; save out the white of one, beat the white of one to a froth, adding a little sugar, and laying it over the top, after baking, to brown it.

LEMON PIE.

Two lemons, grate the peel, and put in the juice; nine spoonsful of sugar, four eggs, one table-spoon of melted butter, half tumbler of milk; beat the yolks and whites separately, add four spoonfuls of sugar to the whites, and put it on top the pie after baked, and set it in the oven to brown the top.

173. MOCK-APPLE PIE.

Two soft crackers, powdered fine, one cup of cold water poured over them, one cup of white sugar, juice of fresh lemon, first grating half the peel, and mix all well together. Bake like apple pie.

174. SQUASH PIE.

Pare, take out the seeds, and stew the squash till very soft and dry; rub it through a sieve or culinder, mix this with good milk till it is as thick as batter, sweeten it with sugar, allow five eggs to a quart of milk, beat the eggs well, add them to the squash, and season with ginger, cinnamon, nutmeg, or whatever spices you like, line a pie plate with crust, fill and bake about an hour.

175. RICE PIE.

Take one pint of boiling water and a small cup of rice. Boil it until very soft, and then take it from the fire, and add a quart of milk, one nutmeg, and six eggs beaten to a froth; add sugar to the taste, and strain it through a sieve. Bake with an under crust, and, if you like, a few raisins.

176. TOMATO PIE.

Pick green tomatoes, pour boiling water over them, and let them remain a few minutes; then strip off the skin, cut the tomatoes in slices, and put them into deep pie-plates. Sprinkle a little ginger and some sugar over them in several layers. Lemon juice and the grated peel improves the pie. Cover the pies with a thick crust, and bake them slowly about an hour.

TOMATO PIE

Cover the bottom with alternate layers of sliced tomatoes, ripe and sound, and bread crumbled fine, with butter and spice to taste; put into a bake-pan with loaf bread, sliced fine, and sprinkle fine sugar over each layer of tomatoes, as it is put in. Cover with sliced bread, and bake as you do other pies.

177. PEACH PIE.

Peaches for pie may be ripe but not soft; pare them, cut them up, and finish as common for apple pies. Unripe peaches may be pared and stewed as is usual for apple tart, and baked in a pie or tart.

178. CORN STARCH PIE.

To one quart of milk put two table-spoonsful of corn starch and two eggs. Sweeten, salt, and season to the taste. Line a pie-plate with a crust, and bake as custard.

179. CHICKEN AND TURKEY PATTIES.

Mince some cold chicken or turkey; put to it some of the

gravy, or if you have none, line your pie-dish with a paste; put in your minced meat; work some flour and butter together, and lay bits all over the meats; then nearly fill the dish with water; season with pepper and salt, and, if liked, a little ground mace; cover with a nice paste, and cook till the crust is done.

180. APPLE PIE.

Line the plate with **plain crust, filled** with sliced apple; then, if the apple is **tart, strew it well with sugar**; sprinkle **over with cinnamon, grate half a nutmeg, cover with a** paste, and bake a long time gently, so that the apples may be done.

The above receipt will answer for almost any ripe fruit pies, except in the matter of spices. Peaches, cherries, plums, and such fruit, require more.

181. CHERRY PIE.

Line a deep pie-dish with the crust, fill with layers of cherries and sugar, seasoned with lemon **and nutmeg**. Red currants are a fine addition. Cover with **a crust, and** bake a long time gently.

182. WHORTLEBERRY PIE.

Line a deep plate with crust; fill with the berries; stew in an abundance of sugar, or it will be quite insipid; add **nutmeg and bake** gently.

183. BERRY PIES.

Put a puff paste on your plates, then berries and **sugar**, with a sprinkle of flour, salt, and a very little butter. **Cover** and bake.

184. SMALL PUFFS.

Make **puff** pastry according **to directions given** in this book. Divide it in two equal proportions, roll one of them quite thin, cut it into small **circular cakes**; put two of them together, and sprinkle flour **between**; roll out the remainder half an inch thick, cut it into narrow strips, and lay **them** round the edge of the circular pieces, so as to form a **rim.** Bake them on buttered tins, in a quick oven, till of a light brown. Fill them, when cool, with jelly, or any small preserved fruit you may happen to have.

185. WASHINGTON PIE.

Three eggs, two cups of flour, one of sugar, two-thirds of a cup of flour. Bake in two separate tins, and put the preserve between when cold.

186. CREAM PIE.

One cup of flour, one of sugar, one tea-spoon of cream tartar, three eggs beat well together; quarter tea-spoon of saleratus in a table-spoonful of hot water; bake it half an hour. Twice this will make three pies.

Cream.—Half a cup of flour, one cup of sugar, two eggs, lemon or other flavoring; add this to a pint of boiling milk, stir till it thickens.

CREAM PIES.

One cup of sugar, one egg, salt, four table-spoonsful of flour, one pint of milk. Boil the milk, beat the eggs, sugar and flour well together, with a little cold milk; then add it to the boiilng milk. This will make two pies. Bake the upper and lower crusts together, when done take off the top crust and fill the pie with the cream.

CAKE.

187. RYE CAKE.

Half a cup of sugar, half a cup of butter, beaten together; three eggs, one pint of sour milk, soda enough to sweeten, one cup of flour, rye meal enough to make a little stiffer than cup cake; fill cups half full.

RYE CAKE.

Four cups of flour, two of rye, table-spoonful of shortening, one tea-spoonful of saleratus, mix with cold water, as stiff as you can stir with a spoon.

CAKES.

RYE CAKE.

One cup of rye, one of flour, one of milk, table-spoonful of butter, same of sugar, one egg. Bake in a pan, or muffin rings.

188. CORN CAKES.

One quart of sour milk, three eggs, half a cup of sugar, one tea-spoon of saleratus, tea-spoonful of soda, meal enough to make a stiff batter, so that it will pour into the pan. It makes two cakes. Corn meal is required.

CORN CAKES.

One quart sour milk, three eggs, half a cup of sugar, one tea-spoonful of saleratus, meal enough to make a stiff batter, so that it will pour into pans. Make two cakes.

189. CORN GRIDDLE CAKES.

Turn one-quart of boiling milk or water on to a pint of Indian meal; when luke warm, add three table-spoonsful of flour, three eggs well beaten, tea-spoonful of salt. Bake on a griddle.

CORN MEAL GRIDDLE CAKES.

Boil a quart of milk, and scald with it as much meal as will make a thick mush. (Yellow meal needs more boiling than white.) When it is partially cool, stir in a table-spoonful of dry yeast, or half a cup of wet yeast, three well-beaten eggs, a tea-spoonful of salt, and two table-spoonsful of wheat flour. Let it stand three or four hours, and bake on a hot soap stone griddle, rubbed with salt. (It will be necessary to rub the griddle with the salted rag between every griddle full of cakes to prevent burning.) Yellow meal is the best.

190. TEA CAKE.

One cup of flour, one of sugar, three eggs, tea-spoonful of cream tartar, one of saleratus. Bake in a quick oven.

TEA CAKE.

One quart of sour milk, half a tea-cup of molasses, a tea spoonful of saleratus; break into the milk two eggs, a little ginger, a little salt, and nutmeg; stir in flour till it becomes a thick batter, then turn it into a well greased pan, and bake twenty minutes.

TEA CAKE.

Three cups of flour, one of sugar, one large spoon of butter, one cup of sour milk, one tea-spoonful of saleratus, one nutmeg, or lemon.

191. TUMBLER CAKE.

Three tumblers of flour, one of sweet milk, quarter tumbler of butter, tea-spoonful of cream tartar, one of saleratus, two eggs.

TUMBLER CAKE.

One tumbler of sugar, one-half tumbler of butter, one-half tumbler of milk, two eggs, one tea-spoonful saleratus, two of cream tartar, flour enough to make it a right thickness, bake about three-quarters of an hour.

192. SPONGE CAKE.

Eight eggs, same weight in sugar, three-quarters pound of flour; beat the yolks and sugar together, whites by themselves, until they will not slip from the spoon; put in the oven as soon as beaten enough.

Or, two cups of flour, two of sugar, six eggs, essence of lemon.

Or, take twelve eggs, two cups of powdered loaf sugar, the grated rind of a lemon, and half its juice; beat to a stiff froth; then add two cups of sifted flour, and bake in a quick oven twenty minutes.

Or, one coffee cup of sugar, four eggs, beat them to a cream; dissolve a small piece of saleratus in a tea-spoonful of milk, add a little nutmeg or essence of lemon; stir in carefully a coffee cup of flour. Bake in a quick oven.

Sponge Cake. — Take one dozen eggs, weigh seven eggs, and take an equal weight of sugar, then weigh five eggs and take an equal weight of flour, now break the eggs, keeping the whites separate, put your sugar into the yolk, grate in the peel of a lemon, then beat it an hour. Put the juice of the lemon into the whites, beat twenty minutes, put half of the whites into the yolks, sift in the flour, stir in the remainder of the whites and bake.

Or four eggs, one coffee cup of sugar, one of flour, half a tea-spoon of cream tartar, a little saleratus, rose water and nutmeg.

193. SEED CAKE.

Beat one pound of butter to a cream, adding gradually a quarter of a pound of sifted sugar, beating both together; have ready the yolks of eighteen eggs, and the whites of ten beat separately; mix in the whites first, then the yolks, and beat the whole for ten minutes; add two grated nutmegs, one pound and a half of flour, and mix very gradually with the other ingredients; when the oven is ready, beat in three ounces of carraway seeds.

Or, four cups of flour, one and a half of cream or milk, half of butter, three eggs, half a cup of seeds, two cups of sugar, a tea-spoonful of saleratus.

Or, two cups of sugar, one of butter, half of cream, one nutmeg, three eggs, one tea-spoonful of saleratus, flour enough to make them roll. Seeds.

194. LEMON CAKE.

Beat six eggs, the yolks and whites separately, till in a solid froth; add to the yolks the grated rind of a fine lemon and six ounces of sugar, dried and sifted; beat this quarter of an hour; shake in with the left hand six ounces of dried flour; then add the whites of the eggs and the juice of the lemon; when these are well beaten in, put it immediately into tins, and bake it about an hour in a moderately hot oven.

Or, one tea-cup of butter, three of sugar, rub them to a

cream, add the yolks of five eggs, well beaten, dissolve a tea-spoonful of soda in a cup of sweet milk; add the juice and peel of one lemon, and the whites of five eggs, four cups of flour.

LEMON LOAF CAKE.

Five eggs, three cups of sugar, one of butter, one of milk, three and a half of flour, a tea-spoon of soda; grate the rind of one lemon, strain the juice, sprinkle a little sugar over the loaves before baking.

LEMON SHEET CAKE.

One cup of butter, three of sugar, yolks of five eggs, one cup of milk, one tea-spoon of soda, the grated peel and juice of one lemon; lastly, add the whites of the eggs, beaten stiff, and four cups of flour sifted in as lightly as possible. Bake in thin sheets.

195. QUEEN CAKE.

Mix one pound of dried flour, the same of sifted sugar, and washed currants; wash one pound of butter in rose-water, beat it well, then mix with it eight eggs, yolks and whites beaten separately, and put in the dry ingredients by degrees; beat the whole an hour; butter little tins, tea-cups, or saucers, filling them only half full; sift a little fine sugar just as you put them into the oven.

196. SHORT CAKE.

Half a pint of flour, lard or butter as large as an egg, tea-spoonful of saleratus dissolved, wet it with cold water, stiff enough to roll well, bake in a quick oven.

THIN SHORT CAKE.

One cup of butter, three of sugar, four eggs, one tea-spoonful of dry saleratus, dissolved in two of water; flour enough to roll out and bake thin.

197. COLD WATER RUSK.

Three cups of flour, two of sugar, three-quarters cup of

butter, three eggs, tea-spoonful of saleratus, and one of cream tartar, dissolved in a cup of water.

198. POUND CAKE.

Mix a pound of sugar with three-quarters of a pound of butter. When well stirred, mix in the yolks of eight eggs, beaten to a froth, then the whites. Add a pound of sifted flour, and mace and nutmeg to the taste. If you wish to have your cake particularly nice, stir in, just before you put it into the pans, a quarter of a pound of citron, or almonds blanched, or powdered fine in rose water.

POUND CAKE.

One pound of sugar, one pound of flour, one pound of butter, and eight eggs; beat it well, and bake three-quarters of an hour.

Or, two and a half pounds of flour, two and a half of sugar, two pounds of butter, nine eggs, two pounds of currants, one nutmeg.

199. PRAIRIE CAKE.

One cup of butter, two of sugar, three eggs, one cup of milk, one tea-spoonful of cream tartar, half a spoonful of saleratus, spice to taste; flour enough to stir up soft.

200. LOUISA SPONGE CAKE.

Five eggs, the weight of four of them in sugar, the weight of three in flour; beat the whites and yolks separately ten minutes, then put the sugar with the eggs, and beat ten minutes; sift the flour, put together as quickly as possible.

201. LOAF CAKE.

Four eggs, five cups of flour, one pound of raisins, two cups of sugar, one cup of molasses, one and a half of butter, one cup of new milk, one tea-spoonful saleratus, spice as you like.

LOAF CAKE.

One cup and a half of butter, three cups of brown sugar,

sifted, one-half cup of molasses, five eggs, two tea-spoons of mace, tea-spoon of clove, have spoon of allspice, one-fourth of a pound of citron, half a pound of currants, five cups of flour, one glass of brandy, half tea-spoon of soda, dissolved and put in the molasses.

202. TEMPERANCE CAKE.

One and a half cups of milk, one and a half cups of sugar, three and a half flour, tea-spoonful of saleratus, spice as you like.

203. INDIAN MEAL PUFFS.

Into one quart of boiling milk, stir eight table-spoonsful of meal, and four table-spoonsful of sugar. Boil five minutes, stirring constantly. When cool, add six well-beaten eggs. Bake in buttered cups half an hour. Try them with a little butter and maple molasses, and see if they are not good.

204. BREAD CAKE.

To one pint of stale bread, crumbed fine, add five eggs, two tea-cups of flour, half a cup of butter, and one quart milk. Scald the bread with the milk. Make in a batter and bake as buckwheat cakes.

BREAD CAKE.

Take as much dough as will make a large loaf of bread, add three cups of sugar, one of butter, three eggs, one tea-spoon of saleratus, spice and fruit to taste. Makes two loaves.

205. RICE CAKE.

Three eggs, and the same weight of ground rice and sugar, mixed and beaten well. Bake quickly in a mould.

Or, one pound ground rice, one and a half cups of butter, one pound of white sugar, six eggs, one lemon peel grated, one-third cup of sweet milk, one-fourth tea-spoon of soda, two table-spoonsful of flour, bake in thin sheets.

Or, one pound of ground rice, one of flour, one table spoonful of soda, two of cream tartar, three half pints of milk, two table-spoonsful of sugar. Salt.

Or, take a tea-cup and a half of boiled rice, warm it with a pint of milk, mix it smooth, then take it from the fire, stir in a pint of cold milk, and a tea-spoonful of salt. Beat four eggs, and stir them in, together with sufficient flour to make it a thick batter.

Or, one cup and a half of boiled rice, warm it with a pint of milk, mix it smooth, then take it from the fire, stir in a pint of cold milk and a tea-spoonful of salt; beat four eggs, and stir them in together with flour enough to make a thick batter.

206. GREEN CORN CAKE.

Mix a pint of grated green corn with three table-spoonfuls of milk, a tea-cup of flour, half a tea-cup of melted butter, one egg, a tea-spoonful of salt, and some pepper. Drop this mixture into hot butter, by the spoonful, let the cakes fry eight or ten minutes. They are nice served up with meat for dinner.

207. COOKIES.

Two cups of sugar, one of butter, three-quarters of a cup of milk, five cups of flour, a tea-spoonful of saleratus, nutmeg.

Or, one cup of sugar, one-half cup of butter, one-half a cup of sour milk, one-half a tea-spoon of soda, half a tea-spoon of mace or nutmeg; flour sufficient for rolling out very thin.

Or, two pounds of flour, one of sugar, half pound of butter, one egg, one cup of cream, one tea-spoonful of saleratus.

Or, one cup of butter, two of sugar, half a cup of milk, one tea-spoonful of saleratus, one egg, stiff enough with flour to roll.

Or, one cup of butter, two of sugar, five of flour, three-quarters of a cup of milk, a little nutmeg, one tea-spoonful of saleratus.

Or, one cup of butter, two and a half of sugar, four eggs, one nutmeg, half a tea-spoonful of saleratus, made hard enough with flour to roll out; work the butter and sugar together, then add the eggs.

CAKES.

208. JUMBLES.

Take a quarter of a pound of flour, a quarter of a pound of powdered loaf sugar, two ounces of butter, rubbed in the flour, two ounces of currants, two eggs. Drop them on tins.

Or, rub to a cream one pound of butter, and one pound of sugar, mix with it two pounds of flour, three eggs, one tea-spoonful of saleratus and eight spoonsful of milk.

Or, add together one pound of nice sugar, two of flour, and spice to the taste; pass them through a sieve; then add four well beaten eggs, and three-quarters of a pound of melted butter, knead well and bake.

209. WASHINGTON CAKE.

One cup of butter, two and a half of sugar, four eggs, one tea-spoonful of saleratus, four cups of flour, and one cup of milk.

Or, one cup of butter, two and a half cups of sugar, four eggs, one tea-spoonful of saleratus, four cups of flour, one cup of milk.

210. BUCKWHEAT CAKES.

Mix the flour with cold water, add a cup of yeast and a little salt; set it in a warm place over night. If it should be sour in the morning, put in a little saleratus; fry them the same as flat-jacks: keep enough to rise the next mess.

Or, take one quart of buck-wheat meal, half a cup of new yeast, a tea-spoonful of saleratus, a little salt, and a sufficient new milk or cold water to make a thick batter. Put it in a warm place to rise. When it has risen sufficiently, bake it on a griddle or in a spider. The griddle must be well buttered, and the cakes are better to be small and thin.

Or, take two pounds of buckwheat flour; add a small saucer full of Indian meal, a little salt, and a tea-cup of yeast. Mix all together with lukewarm water, to a thicker consistency than batter. Put it in a moderately warm place. When ready to bake, if not quite sweet, add a little saleratus, and bake on a griddle well heated.

211. PAN-CAKES.

Take a pint of cream and six new-laid eggs; beat them well together; put in a quarter of a pound of sugar, and one nutmeg, or a little beaten mace, which you please, and so much as will thicken, almost as much as ordinary pan-cake flour batter; your pan must be heated reasonably hot, and wiped with a clean cloth; this done, spread your batter thin over it and fry.

212. DYSPEPSIA CAKE.

Take five cups of flour, two of sugar, two cups of milk, a little salt, and one tea-spoonful of saleratus.

213. INDIAN CAKE.

Take three cups of Indian meal, two cups of flour, one half a tea-cup of molasses, a little salt, one tea-spoonful of saleratus, and mix them with cold water.

Or, mix a quart of Indian meal with a handful of wheat flour, stir a quart of warmed milk, a tea-spoonful of salt, and two spoonfuls of yeast; stir alternately into the milk, the meal and three well beaten eggs; when light, bake as buck-wheat cakes, on a griddle; send them to the table hot. Should the batter sour, stir in a little saleratus dissolved in lukewarm water, letting it set half an hour before baking.

Or, take one pint of Indian meal and one cup of flour, a little salt and ginger, a table-spoonful of molasses, a tea-spoonful of saleratus, sour milk enough to make a stiff batter, bake them on a griddle like buckwheat cakes.

Or, scald a quart of Indian meal, when lukewarm stir in a half pint of flour, half a tea-cup of yeast, and a little salt, fry them in just enough fat to prevent them from sticking to the pan.

Or, take a quart of sifted Indian meal, sprinkle a little salt over it, mix it with scalding water, stirring it well; bake on a tin in a stove oven. Indian Cake is made with butter-milk, or sour milk, with a little cream or butter rubbed into the meal, and a tea-spoonful of saleratus.

Or, a pint and a half of yellow Indian meal sifted, a handful of wheat flour, a quarter of a pound of fresh butter, a quart of milk, four eggs, a very small tea-spoonful of salt; put the milk into a saucepan, cut the butter into it, set over the fire and warm it until the butter is very soft, but not until it melts; then take it off, stir it well till all is mixed and set away to cool; beat four eggs very light, and when the milk is cold, stir them into it alternately with the meal, a little at a time of each; add the salt; beat the whole very hard after it is all mixed, then butter some muffin-rings on the inside, set them in a hot oven, or on a heated griddle, pour some of the butter into each, and bake the muffins well. Send them hot to table, continuing to bake while a fresh supply is wanted. Pull them open with your fingers and eat them with butter, to which you may add molasses or honey.

Or, three cups of meal, one cup of flour, three cups of milk, one tea-spoonful of saleratus, four spoonfuls of molasses, three eggs, and salt.

214. HARD WAFERS.

Take half a pound of butter, half a pound of sugar, three eggs, one table-spoonful of cinnamon, flavor with lemon, and flour enough to make it a thick dough.

215. PLUM CAKE.

Make a cake of two cups of butter, two cups of molasses, two eggs, one cup of milk or buttermilk, one teaspoonful of saleratus, or volatile salts (which is better), a gill of brandy, one tea-spoonful of essence of lemon, and flour to make it a stiff batter; beat it well, then add one pound of raisins stoned and chopped, one pound of currants, well washed and dried by the fire, and one or two quarters of citron. Bake in a quick oven. This is a fine rich cake easily made, and not expensive.

216. CREAM CAKE.

Four cups of flour, two cups of sugar, three cups of cream, and four eggs. Beat it well, and in square tin pans. When cold, cut it in squares. Bake in a quick oven.

Or, one quart of flour, one pint of cream, a little sour cream, one tea-spoonful of saleratus dissolved in the sour cream. If the flour is not made sufficiently wet with the above quantity of cream, add more sweet cream.

Or, boil together half pint of water, half tea-cup of butter, when boiling add one and a half cups of flour, stirring it well; when cool add four eggs, one at a time, stirring each in thoroughly; add one-half tea-spoonful of soda dissolved.

The Cream.—Boil one pint of milk, beat two eggs, one and a half cups of sugar, one cup of flour, together; add to the milk while boiling; then a small piece of butter; flavor to taste.

Or, one pint of milk, one cup of sugar, one of flour, two eggs; flavor with what you like; boil the milk first; beat eggs and sugar; mix in flour, add milk; stir till no lumps.

The Custard.—One quart of milk, two cups of flour, two of sugar, four eggs; boil the milk; while boiling add sugar, flour, and eggs, well beaten; season with lemon. About a large spoonful of the crust dropped into the pan some ways from each other, because they rise so much; one large spoonful of custard to a cake; when baked, cut a hole in the crust and put the cream in.

The Crust.—One pint of water, half pound of butter, twelve ounces of flour, ten eggs; boil the water and butter, and stir in the flour while the water is boiling; then cool it; when cool, add the eggs well beaten, whites and yolks separately.

217. DOUGHNUTS.

One pound of flour, a quarter of a pound of butter, three quarters of brown sugar, rolled fine, one nutmeg, grated, one tea-spoonful of ground cinnamon, one table-spoonful of good yeast; make it into dough with warm milk; sprinkle flour over it, and cover it with a cloth; set it in a warm place to rise for an hour or more. When light, roll it out to half an inch thickness; cut in squares and diamonds. Have a small iron kettle half filled with lard; let it be boiling hot. Drop in a bit of dough to try it; if it is a fine color, drop in more

CAKES.   83

cakes at once; keep the kettle in motion all the time the cakes are in, else the lard will burn. When the cakes are a fine color take them out with a skimmer and lay them on a sieve to drain.

Or, take three eggs, one cup and a half of sugar, one pint of sour milk, a little saleratus, salt and spice, and mould with flour. Mix the articles together an hour before frying the cakes.

Or, one cup of sour milk, one cup of sugar, one tablespoonful of butter, one egg, half a tea-spoonful of saleratus, nutmeg and flour.

Or, two cups of sugar, one of milk, two tea-spoonfuls of cream tartar, one of soda, two eggs, butter the size of an egg, salt and nutmeg.

Or, one cup of sour milk, one of sugar, one table-spoonful of butter, one egg, half tea-spoonful of butter, one egg, half tea-spoonful of saleratus, nutmeg, flour to make it right.

Or, one cup of molasses, one of sugar, one of sour milk, two eggs, one large tea-spoonful of saleratus, one of salt, lard or butter, the size of an egg, flour enough to roll stiff.

218. APPLE FRITTERS.

One pint of milk, two eggs, a little salt, a third tea-spoonful of soda, four sliced apples; mix a little stiffer than flat jacks, fry like pancakes; to be eaten with sugar and cider.

APPLE FRITTERS.

Take four or five tart mellow apples, pare and cut them in slices and soak them in sweetened lemon juice; make a patter of a quart of milk, a quart of flour, eight eggs; grate in the rind of two lemons; add the juice and apples. Drop the batter by the spoonful into hot lard, taking care to have a slice of apple in each fritter.

219. HOE CAKE.

Scald a quart of Indian meal with just sufficient water to make a thick batter, stir in two spoonfuls of butter and two tea-spoonfuls of salt; turn it into a buttered cake pan; bake about half an hour.

HOE CAKE.

Scald a quart of Indian meal with a pint of water; stir in two tea-spoonsful of salt and a little butter melted; when properly mixed, put into a well greased tin, and bake it half an hour.

220. CRULLERS.

Half a cup of butter, two of sugar, half do. of milk, three eggs; spice to your taste; make hard with flour; fry in hot lard.

Or, one cup of sugar, three eggs, one spoonful of butter; mix stiff with flour.

Or, three eggs, one cup of sugar, one spoonful of butter; mix stiff with flour.

Or, two cups of sugar, half cup of butter, three eggs, half cup of milk; spice to taste; mix hard with flour.

221. GINGER NUTS.

Half a pound of flour, half pound sugar, half a pound butter, half pint of milk, half tea-cup of ginger, half tea-cup of molasses, one tea-spoonful of saleratus.

GINGER SNAPS.

Take one-pint of molasses, one tea-cup of butter, one spoonful of ginger, and one spoonful of saleratus; and boil all the ingredients thoroughly; when nearly cold, add as much flour as can be rolled into the mixture.

Or, mix four ounces of lard, and four of butter, melted with four ounces of brown sugar, a pint of molasses, two tea-spoonsful of ginger, and a quart of flour. Strain in two tea-spoonsful of saleratus, dissolved in a wine-glass of milk, adding sufficient flour for rolling out thin. Cut into small cakes, and bake in a slow oven.

Or, three cups of sugar, three eggs, one cup of butter, half a cup of ginger, one cup of milk, one tea-spoonful of saleratus.

GINGER COOKIES.

Take one tea-cup of sugar, one of molasses, one egg, one spoonful of saleratus, one of ginger, and one of vinegar, and mix them with seven tea-cups of flour.

222. MUFFINS.

Mix a quart of wheat flour smoothly with a pint and a half of luke-warm milk, half a tea-cup of yeast, a couple of beaten eggs, a heaping tea-spoonful of salt, and a couple of table-spoonfuls of luke-warm melted butter. Set the batter in a warm place to rise. When light, butter your muffin cups, turn in the mixture, and bake the muffin till a light brown.

Or, one cup of milk, three table-spoonsful of sugar, piece of butter the size of an egg, two tea-spoonsful of cream tartar, one of soda, three eggs, salt to rise them; mix them over night, and use half a cup of yeast in place of cream tartar and soda.

Or, one quart of milk, butter the size of an egg, two tea-spoonsful of yeast. Salt and flour.

Soda Muffins. — To two pounds of flour, add one tea-spoonful of soda, one of cream tartar, and a tea-spoonful of sugar, a little salt; mix thoroughly, and make into a stiff batter with some milk; beat well for a few minutes. Have ready a hot earthen pan, well buttered, also rings for the purpose. Pour in the batter nearly half an inch thick. Bake a nice brown on each side.

Indian Meal Muffins.—To a quart of meal pour boiling water, stirring constantly, until a thick batter; let it cool; while warm, add a small tea-cup of butter, a tea-spoonful of salt, and a table-spoonful of yeast, with two well-beaten eggs; set it in a warm place for two hours, then stir it smooth, and bake in small cakes on a griddle; when one side is a rich brown, turn the other; lay them singly on a hot dish and serve. These may be made without the yeast, and baked as soon as mixed.

223. GOLD CAKE.

One cup of sugar, half cup of butter, the yolks of eight eggs, half a cup of sweet milk, one tea-spoonful cream tartar, half a tea-spoonful of soda, two cups of flour, and half a nutmeg.

SILVER CAKE.

One and a half cups of sugar, three-quarters cup of sweet milk, three cups of flour, one tea-spoonful cream tartar, half of soda, the whites of eight eggs, one tea-spoonful essence of lemon.

224. COCOA-NUT CAKE.

Four tea-cups of powdered sugar, one cup of butter, four cups of flour, one good sized cocoa-nut, grated fine, one cup sour milk, small tea-spoonful of soda, six eggs, one lemon-peel grated. The amount of flour depends on the thickness of the cocoa-nut. After mixing, bake a very little to try it. If too soft, add more flour.

Or, one pound of cocoa-nut, one of sugar, half pound of butter, half pound of flour, six eggs.

Or, break a cocoa-nut in pieces, lay it in cold water, cut off the rind, and grate the white on a coarse grater; put the whites of four eggs, with half a pound of white sugar, powdered; beat them till very light and white; add to it some essence of lemon and grated cocoa-nut, until it as thick as you can stir it easily with a spoon; lay them in heaps about the size of a nutmeg, on a sheet of paper, let them be placed at least an inch a part; lay the paper on a baking tin, bake them in a quick oven; when they begin to look yellowish, they are done. Let them remain on the paper till they are perfectly cold.

Or, one cup of butter, three of sugar, one of milk, four of flour, before sifted, four eggs, one tea-spoon of cream tartar, half spoon of soda, one cocoa-nut grated fine.

CAKES.

225. OYSTER CORN CAKE.

Take one quart of green corn, rasped with a coarse grater, two cups of new milk, **one** tea-cup of flour; mix the batter together, add two eggs, well beaten **up**; season the batter with salt and pepper, and bake upon a griddle. These cakes afford as good an imitation of the taste of oysters, as can be made with salsify. The corn should be such as is most suitable for roasting or boiling.

226. WESTERN CAKE.

Three cups of sugar, two of butter, **six** eggs, one-half **tea** cup **of** sour milk, one tea-spoonful of soda, one-half **pound** raisins, one-half pound citron, **one tea-cup** of currants. Stir in flour till quite stiff.

227. COMMON CAKE.

Two eggs, one cup of each **of** butter and sugar, **one** and a half cups of molasses, one tea-spoon of saleratus, one cup of sweet or sour milk, half a tea-spoonful of all kinds of spice; flour to make it right.

228. CIDER CAKES.

Three cups of sugar, one cup of butter, **four eggs**, two cups **of** cider, two small tea-spoonsful of soda, tea-spoon of clove and cinnamon; flour to make as stiff as pound cake; chopped raisins; bake in loaf.

229. ONE EGG CAKE.

One cup of sour milk, one tea-spoonful of saleratus, **one** cup and a half of sugar, butter the size of an egg, **one egg**, flavor with lemon; flour enough to make it right.

230. FROSTING **FOR WEDDING CAKE.**

The whites of ten eggs, six pounds of sugar, one tea-cup of starch, pulverized, and four lemons.

Or, the weight of fifteen eggs in sugar, to six beaten to a froth; put one pint of water to the sugar, boil it to a candy, or until it will string from a knife; then pour it gently upon the egg while hot, stirring all the time; continue to beat it till stiff enough to drop from a spoon, slowly. Flour the cakes, and wipe off the crumbs; put it on so thick as not to frost it but once.

231. GINGERBREAD.

One and three-quarters pound of flour, one pint of molasses, **one** tea-spoonful of saleratus dissolved in a cup of **milk, one** spoonful of ginger, quarter pound of butter.

Hard Gingerbread. **Two cups of molasses, one of butter,** half a tea-spoonful **of saleratus, table-spoon of ginger,** salt, stiff enough with flour to roll.

Imperial Gingerbread. — Rub **six ounces** of butter into three-quarters of a pound of flour; them mix six ounces of **treacle with a pint** of cream carefully, lest it **should turn the cream; mix in a quarter** of a pound of double-refined sugar, half an ounce of powdered ginger, and one ounce of carraway seeds; stir the whole well together in a paste, cut it into shapes, and stick cut candied orange or lemon peel on the top.

232. PORK CAKE.

One pound salt pork, chopped **fine, one** cup of boiling water poured over it, three cups of molasses, one tablespoon of soda, three eggs, flour to make as pound cake, one **pound of currants, one** pound of raisins; spice.

233. HARRISON CAKE.

Five cups of flour, **one and** a half of butter, two and a half of molasses, four **eggs,** one table-spoon of cloves, one **tea-spoon of** saleratus, **two** pounds of stoned raisins, a handful of Indian meal, sifted; bake slow.

234. COFFEE CAKE.

One cup **of** sugar, **one** of molasses, one of butter, one of coffee, half tea-spoonful **of** saleratus, all kinds of spice, one **cup** of chopped **raisins; mix all** together, stiffness of gingerbread.

PUDDINGS AND SAUCES.

OBSERVATIONS ON MAKING PUDDINGS.

The cloths used to tie over puddings, or boil them in, should be nicely washed and dried in the sun, and kept in a dry place. When to be used, they should be dipped into boiling water, squeezed dry and floured. In all cases the eggs must be thoroughly beaten. If bread pudding, the cloth should be tied loose, to give room for rising. If batter, tight over. The water should boil quick when the pudding is put in, and it should be moved about for a minute, that the ingredients should mix evenly. Batter pudding should be strained through a coarse sieve when all mixed. In others, strain the eggs separately. The pans must always be buttered before the pudding is put in. A pan of cold water must be ready, and the pudding dipped in, as soon as it comes out of the pot; then it will not adhere to the cloth.

235. TRANSPARENT PUDDING.

Eight eggs, eight ounces of butter, eight ounces of sugar, one nutmeg, grated. Beat up the eggs, put them into the stew-pan with the sugar and butter, nutmeg to taste; set it on a stove or fire of coals, stirring it constantly until it thickens, then pour it into a basin to cool. Set a rich paste round the edge of your dish, pour in your pudding, and bake it in a moderate oven. A most delicious and elegant article.

236. CHESHIRE PUDDING.

One pound of raspberry jam, one cup of cream of buttermilk, one table-spoonful of saleratus, four ounces of butter, one and a half pounds of flour. Rub the half of the butter into the flour, warm the milk, rub the saleratus fine with the broad blade of a knife on the corner of a paste-board, then scrape it in, and while it is effervesence, mix with the flour and the rest of the butter, and a dust of more salt if necessary, then roll out to fourteen or fifteen inches long, and eight or nine in width; spread with the jam, and roll it up in the manner of collared eel; have a floured cloth ready and wrap it two or three times around and pin it; tie it tight at each end. Boil in plenty of water two hours. Serve with thickened sweet sauce, with some rose-water and nutmeg, and juice of a lemon.

Nice stewed peaches are fine in this dumpling, with cream sweetened, and nutmeg for sauce. Almost any acid fruit is excellent in this way. The crust should be light, and it must be eat as soon as done.

237. TAPIOCA PUDDING.

One quart of milk, seasoning, five eggs, one coffee cup of tapioca. Steep the tapioca in the milk two hours, put it in cold, let it warm a little, beat up the eggs well with sufficient sugar, a little essence of lemon. Bake half an hour, eat with butter.

Or, pick and wash four table-spoonsful of tapioca, and pour upon it a pint of scalding milk. Let it stand half an hour, then add a pint of cold milk, two eggs, sugar, spice, and raisins, if you like.

238. QUINCE PUDDING.

Scald the quinces tender, pare them thin, scrape off the pulp, mix with sugar, very sweet, and add a little ginger and cinnamon. To a pint of cream put three or four yolks of eggs, and stir it into the quinces till they are of a good thickness. Butter the dish, pour it in, and bake it.

239. BAKED POTATO PUDDING.

Twelve ounces of boiled potatoes, skinned and mashed, one ounce of cheese grated fine, one ounce of suet, one gill of milk. Mix the potatoes, suet, milk, cheese, all together; if not of a proper consistence, add a little water. Bake it in an earthen pan.

Or, boil one quart of potatoes quite soft, and then rub them smooth through a hair sieve. Have ready half a pound of melted butter and six eggs, beat light; mix the butter with half a pound of sugar; stir in the eggs, adding half a pound of currants; put the mixture into a thick cloth, and boil it half an hour. To be eaten with wine sauce.

240. ALMOND PUDDING.

One pound of blanched almonds, one-half a glass of rose water, six eggs, eight ounces of sugar, one-pint of cream. Put the rose-water to the almonds in a marble mortar, pound them fine; beat the sugar and eggs together well, the sugar being nicely sifted; put all into a basin, and stir them over a few coals, well together, until they are warm, then put it into a thin dish, put paste only around the edges, (or sides of the dish,) bake three-quarters of an hour.

241. CUSTARD PUDDING.

One quart of milk, six eggs, six spoonsful of flour, one nutmeg, sugar and butter. Boil the milk, and while scalding, stir in the flour; set to cool half an hour before it is wanted, beat up the eggs nicely, and put to the milk with sufficient salt, bake in a quick oven twenty minutes. Rub nutmeg, with nice sugar and butter for sauce.

Or, one quart of milk, eight eggs, half a pound of sugar, season with lemon or peach, pour it into a pudding dish wet with cream, and set the pudding into a pan half filled with water, and put them into the oven to bake for three-quarters of an hour. If preferred, line the baking dish with delicate cream paste. Less eggs will make a good custard.

Or, take a pint of milk, four spoonsful of flour, six eggs, spice to your taste and bake.

242. FLOUR PUDDING.

One pint of milk, six eggs, six spoonsful of flour. Boil the milk, stir in the flour whilst scalding, let it cool; have the water boiling. When sufficiently cool, beat the eggs well, and put them in with salt to taste; boil hard one hour. Rub nutmeg with nice sugar and butter for sauce.

Or, beat two eggs and a little milk, and stir in five table-spoonsful of flour, making a batter. Boil one quart of milk, and when it boils, pour in the butter, stirring well, while it is poured in. Let it boil slowly for a few minutes. Eat it with sweetened cream or milk, or whatever sauce suits you best. It is a cheap, quick way of making a very pleasant and wholesome dessert. Wheat meal, unbolted flour, can be used instead of flour.

Or, one quart of milk, five eggs, nine tea-spoonsful of flour, braided sugar and butter for sauce.

243. SAGO PUDDING.

Four spoonsful of sago, one and a half pints of milk, four eggs, lemon peel, cinnamon, nutmegs, and sugar to taste. Boil the milk and sago nicely, let it cool; beat the eggs up perfectly with some sugar; add the ingredients, then mix all together, put a nice paste round the dish, pour in the pudding, and bake slowly.

Pick, wash and dry, half a pound of currants; and put in such spices as best suit the taste of those who are to eat it. Have ready six table-spoonsful of sago, picked clean, and soaked for two hours in cold water. Boil the sago in a quart of milk till quite soft. Then stir alternately into the milk, a quarter of a pound of butter, and six ounces of powdered sugar, and set it away to cool. Beat eight eggs, and when they are quite light stir them gradually into the milk, sago, &c. Add the spice, and lastly the currants, having dredged them well with flour to prevent their sinking. Stir the whole very hard, put it into a buttered dish, and bake it three-quarters of an hour. It may be eaten cold.

Or, boil five table-spoonsful of sago, well picked and

washed, in a quart of milk, till quite soft, with **a stick of cinnamon.** Then stir in one tea-cup of butter, and two of powdered loaf sugar. When it is cold, add six eggs **well** beaten, and a little grated nutmeg. Mix all well together, and bake in a buttered dish three-quarters of an hour. Brown sugar, if dried, will **answer** very well **to sweeten it.**

244. BOILED CUSTARD PUDDING.

One pint of new **milk, two spoonsful of flour,** yolks of five eggs, orange-flower water, cinnamon, currant jelly. Mix the flour with the milk by degrees; beat the yellows and other ingredients, with a little **salt together, and put with** the milk. Butter a basin that will exactly hold it, pour the batter in, and tie a floured **cloth over it.** Put in a kettle of boiling water, and **turn it about a few minutes, to prevent** the eggs from settling on one side. Half an hour will boil it. Pour currant jelly over, and serve with sweet sauce.

245. RICE PUDDING.

One quart of milk, **four ounces of rice,** one-half nutmeg, one stick of cinnamon, four spoonsful of rose water, eight eggs, salt. Boil the rice and cinnamon with the milk, stir it often to keep it from burning, cool, add the nutmeg and other ingredients, having beat the eggs well. Butter a pan or dish, or cover the dish with puff paste; pour the composition in, bake one hour and a half. Serve with butter and sugar.

Or, one pint of cooked rice, one pint of milk, one teaspoonful of salt, and the yolks of four eggs. Bake till done, then add the whites of four eggs, beaten to a froth, with four table-spoonsful of sugar. Bake again five minutes. Serve with liquid sauce.

Or, half a cup of rice, cover it with milk, and boil it a little, butter a dish, put in three pints of milk, one tea-spoonful of flour or corn starch, while it is in the oven; sugar and nutmeg. Bake one hour. If the crust form too brown, **take** it off before it is done.

RICE PUDDING, BAKED OR BOILED.

Wash in cold water, and pick very clean, six ounces of rice; boil it in one quart of milk, with a bit of cinnamon, very gently, till it is quite tender; it will take about an hour; be careful to stir it often. Take it from the fire, pick out the cinnamon, and stir in a tea-cupful of sugar, half a cup of butter, three eggs well beaten, a little powdered nutmeg; stir it till it is quite smooth. You can line a pie-dish with puff-paste, or bake it in a buttered dish, which is better; three-quarters of an hour will bake it.

If you wish it more like custard, add one more egg, and half a pint of milk.

If you boil it, you can add whatever fruit you like; three ounces of currants, or raisins, or apples minced fine; it will take an hour to boil it. Serve with wine sauce or butter and sugar.

GROUND RICE PUDDING.

Add to one pint of milk four eggs well beaten, and one and a half table-spoonsful of ground rice; boil these together, stirring them. Pour the mixture, while hot, over two ounces of butter, sugar to the taste, and add the grated rind with the juice of a middle sized lemon. Line the dish with puff paste before putting in the mixture, and bake.

BAKED RICE PUDDING.

One cup of rice, one of molasses, two quarts of milk, one egg, salt and spice.

246. BOSTON APPLE PUDDING.

Eighteen good apples four yolks of eggs, one white, one lemon, one-half nutmeg, one-quarter pound of butter, cinnamon, cloves, sugar to taste. Peel, core, and cut the apples, into a stew-pan that will just hold them, with a little water and the spices, rasp the peel of the lemon in, stew over a slow fire till quite soft, then sweeten and pass through a sieve, beat the eggs and grated nutmeg together, with the juice of a lemon, them mix all well, line the inside of your pie-dish with good puff paste, put in your pudding, bake half an hour

PUDDINGS.

APPLE PUDDING DUMPLING.

Put into a nice paste, quartered apples, tie up in a floured cloth, and boil two hours; serve with sweet sauce.

Pears, plums, peaches, &c, are fine done this way.

Or, pare and stew two quarts of apples, mash them, add eight eggs, half a pound of butter, sugar and nutmeg, or grated lemon peel, and bake on short crust.

Or, peel and core six very large apples, stew them in six table-spoonsful of water, with the rind of a lemon; when soft, beat them to a pulp, add six ounces of good brown sugar, six well-beaten eggs, a pint of rich cream, and a teaspoonful of lemon juice; line a dish with puff paste, and when baked, stick all over the top thin chops of candied citron and lemon-peel.

247. INDIAN PUDDING.

Three pints of milk, seven eggs, one-half pound of raisins, one-quarter pound of butter, seven spoonsful of Indian meal, spice, salt, and sugar to the taste. Scald the milk, and stir it in the meal whilst boiling; set it to cool, stone and put in the raisins, salt and spice; then beat the eggs well, and if only milk-warm, put them in, stir all well together, bake an hour and a half good heat.

Or, sift a pint of Indian meal, and scald it with boiling water. Place over the fire a quart of milk, cut up a quarter of a pound of butter, and melt it in the hot milk, add a pint of sugar-house molasses, and mix them together until the milk boils. Stir it into the meal, mixing it well with a wooden spoon. Beat seven eggs, until they are perfectly light, pour them into the bowl that holds the meal, with ten drops of the essence of lemon, or a little lemon juice.

Stir the mixture till it seems quite light, and bake it in a moderately hot oven.

Or, one quart of sour milk, a tea-spoonful of saleratus, half a cup of molasses, a tea-cupful of chopped suet, meal enough to make it stiff.

Or, take one pint of milk, and one-quarter of a pound of Indian meal, and boil it smooth; then add one-quarter and half a quarter of a pound of butter, and half a pound of sugar. When cool, beat in the yolks of six eggs; beat the whites of the eggs to a froth and add them last. Put in spice to your liking. Bake the mixture on shallow plates.

Boiled Indian Pudding. — Take sweet milk, stir into it fine corn meal sifted, until as thick as can be conveniently stirred with a spoon: add a little salt, some berries; put the batter thus prepared into a bag made of strong linen or cotton cloth, not quite full, because the meal will swell; tie the bag with a strong cord; put it directly into boiling water; let it boil as fast as possible for three hours; serve up with sauce, which may be made of cream and sugar.

248. LEMON PUDDING.

One-half pound of sugar, one-half pound best butter, one lemon, five eggs, one glass of rose water, one glass orange-flower water. Beat the rose-water and butter to a froth, prepare the sugar and eggs as for pound cake, grate the yellow part of the lemon rind in, (but not a particle of white,) have a nice puff paste ready in your dish, and, after incorporating the pudding well together, pour it into your paste. Bake in a moderate oven. Orange pudding is made in the same way, using a pounded orange instead of a lemon.

Or, beat together three-quarters of a pound of sugar, one half a pound of butter, five eggs, beaten to a froth, two large spoonsful grated bread, the juice of one lemon, and half the rind grated. Bake in plates, with paste below.

Or, half a pound of bread crumbs, quarter of a pound of suet, quarter of a pound of brown sugar, one lemon, juice and rind, and one egg; to be boiled in a mould one hour. Serve with a little wine sauce, if approved.

Or, half a pound of flour, half a pound of suet cut very fine, half a pound of crushed sugar, the rind of two lemons, and the juice, and one or two eggs; boil it four hours in a shape. Served up without sauce, it is excellent.

249. VERMICELLI PUDDING.

Four ounces of vermicelli, five yolks, three whites eggs, one pint of milk, lemon peel, cinnamon, loaf sugar, salt to taste. Boil the milk, with the lemon peel grated in, sweeten and strain through a sieve, put in the vermicelli, boil ten minutes, cool, have the eggs well beaten; when sufficiently cool, put them into the pudding, mix well together, and steam one hour and a quarter, or bake half an hour.

Or, soak four ounces of vermicelli in cold water for one hour; pour the water off, put on the fire with a quart of sweet milk, shake it till it boils, draw it aside until the milk is all soaked in. Beat up four eggs, with two ounces of sugar; mince two ounces of lemon peel. Mix all together, and bake in a pudding dish. If boiled, it will require six eggs instead of four. Put in a buttered shape and boil two hours.

250. SUET PUDDING.

Four ounces of suet, one-half pint of milk, three tablespoons of flour, two eggs, one spoon of ginger. Mince the suet fine, and roll it thin, salt it, mix well with the flour; beat the eggs well, and mix with milk and spices; flour a cloth that has been dipped into boiling water, tie it loose, put into boiling water, boil hard an hour and a quarter. Serve with sweetened sauce, with the squeeze of a lemon in it.

Or, one cup of suet, one of molasses, one of milk, one teaspoonful of soda, one of cloves, and one of allspice, half a nutmeg, one cup of raisins; mix with flour enough for a stiff batter, boil it three hours. For sauce, egg, sugar and butter.

251. SPRING PUDDING.

Four dozen sticks of rhubarb, (or pie-plant,) one lemon, one-half pound of loaf sugar, one spoon of cinnamon. Wash and peel the rhubarb, cut short, throw it into a stew pan with the grated rind of the lemon, and cinnamon, and sugar; set it to cook, reduce it to a marmalade, pass it through a hair sieve, have a pie-dish lined with a good puff paste, and pour the pudding in; bake half an hour.

252. BATTER PUDDING.

Six ounces of flour, three eggs, salt, one pint of milk. Have the milk boiled, and beat the eggs well; add milk until it is smooth, the thickness of cream, mix all well together, then have a dish buttered that **will just** hold it; or it is nice to boil as before directed. Boil **one and a** half, **or** two hours.

Or, beat two eggs and a little milk, and **stir in** five tablespoonsful of flour, making **a** batter. Boil one **quart of** milk, and when it boils, pour in the butter, stirring well while it **is** poured in. Let it boil slowly for a few minutes. Eat it with sweetened cream or **milk, or** whatever sauce suits best your palate. It is a cheap, quick way, of making a very pleasant and wholesome dessert. Wheat meal, unbolted flour, can be used instead of flour.

253. BREAD PUDDING.

Four eggs, one pint of **milk, one** pint **crumbs of** bread, one stick **of** cinnamon, sugar, nutmeg, salt to taste. Boil the bread **and milk** with the cinnamon ten minutes, then cool, pass through **a** sieve, beat the eggs very well, and add **to** the batter, sweeten and salt, mix well together, bake half **an** hour; or, boil one hour and **a** quarter.

Baked Bread Pudding. — Broken pieces of bread are **good soaked** in milk until soft, then add two eggs to a quart, **a** little **salt,** butter, lemon-peel, nutmeg, or cinnamon, and **sugar.** Bake an hour. This is wholesome, and best **for common use.**

Or, half a pound **of** stale bread crumbs, one pint and a **half** of boiling milk, poured over **six** eggs, beat light, and **added when** the milk **cools,** a quarter of a pound of butter, **a quarter of a pound of** brown **sugar,** one nutmeg, and **three-quarters of a pound** of currants. Melt the butter in **the milk, beat the eggs and** sugar together, and butter the **dish in which the pudding is** to be baked.

254. CHRISTMAS PUDDING.

Chop half a pound of beef suet very fine, stone and chop one pound of raisins; wash, pick, clean from grit, and dry, a pound of currants; soak half of a sixpenny loaf of bread in a pint of milk; when it has taken up all the milk, add to it the raisins, currants, chopped suet, and two eggs beaten, a table-spoonful of sugar, one wine-glass of brandy, one nutmeg grated, and any other spice that may be liked. Boil four hours. For sauce, beat a **quarter of** a pound of butter to a cream, then **stir into it half a** pound of powdered loaf sugar. Or, melt butter and sugar, and if liked, add more brandy.

Or, one pound of raisins, stoned, one pound of currants, half a pound of beef suet, quarter of a pound of sugar, two spoonsful of flour, three eggs, a **cup** of sweetmeats, and **a** wine-glass of brandy. Mix well **and** boil in a mould eight hours.

255. PLUM PUDDING.

Take half a pound of flour, half a pound of **raisins stoned** and chopped, and some currants washed, picked and dried; use milk enough to stir easily with a spoon; add half a pound **of suet** chopped **fine, a** tea-spoonful of salt, and four well beaten eggs; tie in **a floured** cloth, and boil **four** hours. The **water** must boil when it is put in, and **continue boiling** until it is done.

BAKED PLUM PUDDING.

Take one loaf of **baker's bread, broken** up, (save the crust,) and pour over it three pints of **warm milk,** and let it stand for an hour. While warm, put **in a piece** of butter as large as an egg, half a pound **of** raisins, **six** eggs, and half **a** pound of currants, adding citron, nutmeg, and any thing else **you** please. Bake it three hours, and eat it with wine sauce.

PERPETUAL PLUM PUDDING.

Three pounds of stoned raisins, three pounds **of** brown sugar, three pounds of currants, three pounds of grated bread, three pounds of suet, shred fine, three pounds of eggs, one pound of citron, three table-spoonsful of flour, quarter of a pint of wine, quarter of **a** pint of brandy, two nutmegs, a little mace, and a tea-spoonful of salt. Mix the ingredients well together, and divide into six equal parts; tie each part in a separate cloth; put them in water already boiling, and boil four hours. If they are to be kept, hang them in a cool place, and when wanted for use, boil them again from one to three hours, according to the time they have been hanging.

256. RYE PUDDING.

Five table-spoonsful of rye meal, and one pint of milk, well beaten, one small table-spoonful of butter, a little salt; boil in a bag one hour.

Or, a table-spoonful of rye-meal, one pint of milk, well beaten; one small table-spoonful of melted butter; salt; boil in a bag one hour.

257. APPLE CUSTARD PUDDING.

Take apple pared, cored, and slightly stewed, sufficient to cover the dish, eight eggs, one quart of milk, spice to your taste, bake it one-third of an hour.

258. BIRD'S NEST PUDDING.

Put into three **pints of** boiling milk, six crackers pounded **fine, and one** pint **of raisins.** When **cool, add four** eggs, **well** beaten, **a** little sugar, **and** five good sized apples, pared, **with the core** carefully **removed.** To be eaten with warm sauce.

259. BERRY PUDDING.

One quart of flour, one and half tea-spoonful saleratus, **two** tea-spoonsful cream tartar, dry; stir in the berries and **wet them** with milk and a little water; boil in a bag. *Sauce for same.*—One **cup of** molasses, one cup of sugar, and a piece **of butter two-thirds** as large as an egg; boil **up** and pour into a bowl; add a little nutmeg.

Or, one quart of flour, one and a half tea-spoonful of saleratus, and two tea-spoonsful of cream tartar, dry; stir in the berries and wet them up with milk and a little water; boil in a bag.

260. SUET PUDDING.

One cup suet, one do. molasses, one do. milk, one tea-spoonful soda, one of cloves, and one of allspice, half a nutmeg, one cup of raisins, mix with flour enough for a stiff batter, boil it three hours. For sauce—egg, sugar and butter.

Or, 4 ounces of suet, half pint of milk, three table-spoonsful of flour, two eggs, one spoonful of ginger. Mince the suet fine and roll it thin, salt it, and mix well with the flour, beat the eggs well, and mix with milk and spices; flour a cloth that has been dipped into boiling water, tie it loose, put it into boiling water, boil hard an hour and a quarter. Serve with sweetened sauce, with the squeeze of a lemon in it.

261. COTTAGE PUDDING.

One cup sweet milk, three do. of flour, one of sugar, one table-spoonful melted butter, half tea-spoonful of soda, one egg. Baked about half an hour.

Or, one tea-cup of sugar, one of milk, two heaping cups of flour, three table-spoonsful of melted butter, one egg, one tea-spoonful of soda, one do. of cream tartar. If made of sour milk, omit the cream.

262. ENGLISH PLAIN PUDDING.

One loaf of bread, two quarts of milk, ten eggs, one pound of suet, two ounces of citron, two pounds of raisins, two pounds of currants, one cup of brandy, one of sugar, one of molasses, one tea-spoonful of cloves, one of cinnamon, one nutmeg. Tie in a cloth and boil two hours.

263. CORN PUDDING.

Six ears of sweet corn, one quart of milk, two table-spoonsful of flour, three eggs, sugar and salt, to taste; cut the corn through the center, then cut it off. Bake one hour.

264. ARROW ROOT PUDDING.

From a quart of new milk take a small tea-cup full, and mix it with two large tea-spoonsful of arrow root; boil the remainder of the milk, and stir it amongst the arrow root; add, when nearly cold, four well beaten eggs, with two ounces of pounded loaf sugar and the same of fresh butter broken into small bits; season with grated nutmeg; mix it well together, and bake it in a buttered dish fifteen or twenty minutes.

Or, wet three table-spoonsful of arrow root in a little milk, add one or two well beaten eggs, boil one quart of milk; when boiled pour the above mixture into it all the time. Let it boil five minutes. This should be eaten cold like blanc mange with sugar and cream.

265. CRACKER PUDDING.

Eight crackers, pour over one quart of new milk, and let stand over night; four eggs; raisins; if a little stiff, add a little more milk.

266. COCOA NUT PUDDING.

One quart of milk, six eggs, one cocoa nut, large, one table-spoonful of flour, one of butter, sugar to taste. Bake in crust.

267. PINE APPLE PUDDING.

Peel and grate one Pine Apple, take the weight in sugar, half its weight in butter; rub them to a cream; then stir in the apple, five eggs, one cup of cream, salt. Bake one hour, with or without a crust.

268. PUDDING SAUCE.

One pint of sugar, a table-spoonful of vinegar, a piece of butter the size of an egg; boil fifteen minutes; add a little nutmeg; boil with the sugar in nearly a pint of water, a large table-spoonful of flour.

Or, boil some orange or lemon peel, or some peach leaves, in half a pint of water; take them out and pour in a thin paste, made with two spoonsful of flour, and boil five minutes, then add a pint of brown sugar and let it boil; then put in two spoonsful of butter, and take it up immediately.

DOMESTIC WINES.

269. GRAPE WINE.

To each gallon of bruised perfectly ripe grapes add a gallon of water, and let the whole stand a week; then draw off the liquor, and put to every gallon three pounds of best sugar; when fermentation in a temperate situation is about over, stop it close. Bottle it in about six months.

270. CURRANT WINE.

Put together the same measurement of good ripe currants, and pure water; mash the currants till reduced to a pulp; strain through a thick woolen bag. Put it in a barrel, with four pounds of sugar to every gallon of juice, leaving sufficient space in the barrel for the liquor to ferment. Bung it close, and set it away in a cool place to ferment. Rack it off in November following, bottle it up, when it is fit for use —improves with age.

Or, one gallon of water, one quart of currant juice, and three pounds of sugar. This will make a pleasantly vinous drink, not in the least *heady*, and very refreshing in a hot day. It will keep as long as it is bottled tight and improves by age. We have used it a long time, and though it may not be equal to "native wine," so called, yet every one who drinks of it pronounces it delicious.

Or, squeeze the fresh, but fully ripe berries, till the juice ceases to run freely. Pour over the pulp as much water as there is juice, and press again. Repeat the process, which will extract all the juice and form a liquid of the proper consistence, viz: two parts water and one part juice. Add one-third of its weight of white sugar, and place in wide, open vessels, in a moderately cool place, to ferment. In two or three days it will be ready for bottling. Great care is required that the fermentation be not rapid, tending to form vinegar. When this is the case, place in a cooler position. It is sometimes desirable to have the fermentation go on quite slowly, in which case put it in casks, leaving the bung open and keep in a cool place for a week, or two even, before drawing off or bottling. Add cloves or cinnamon to flavor it, if you desire.

Or, bruise the currants, and to each gallon of the juice add equal weight of sugar, and to each gallon of this liquid add a gallon of water; put it into a cask, and in about twenty days add brandy in proportion of a pint to fifteen gallons. Bottle in March.

271. ELDERBERRY WINE.

Fill the kettle with water even with the berries; boil till the berries are soft; then strain them and squeeze out the juice. To five quarts of juice add six pounds of sugar; then boil the syrup; when cool add yeast enough to have it ferment; then skim and boil again; when cool it is ready for bottling.

272. RHUBARB WINE.

One gallon of juice, three gallons of water, twelve pounds best sugar, one slice of bread, toasted, soaked in yeast.

273. COTTAGE BEER.

Take a peck of fresh wheat-bran, put into ten gallons water, with three handfuls of hops; boil the whole together in a brass or copper kettle, until the bran and hops sink to the bottom. Then strain it through a hair sieve or a thin sheet into a cooler, and when lukewarm, add two quarts of molasses. As soon as the molasses is melted, pour the whole into a ten gallon cask, with two table-spoonsful of yeast;

when the fermentation has subsided bung it close. **Tap in four days.**

274. GINGER BEER.

A gallon of boiling water is poured over three-quarters of a pound of loaf sugar, one ounce of ginger, and the peel of one lemon; when milk-warm, the juice of the lemon and a spoonful of yeast are added. It should be made in the evening, and bottled next morning, in stone bottles, and the cork tied down with twine. Good brown sugar will answer, and the lemon may be omitted, if *cheapness* is required.

275. HOP BEER.

For a half barrel of beer, take half a pound of hops and a tea-cupful of ginger; boil it in a pailful and a half of water. When brewed, put it warm into a clean cask, with two quarts of molasses; shake it well, and fill the cask with water, leaving the bung open. Fill the cask when it works over.

276. MEAD.

Three pounds cheap sugar, three pints boiling water, two ounces tartaric acid. After all mixed, bring it to a boil; after boiling add essence lemon, spruce or any flavor you like; put away in bottles; put in a tumbler of water, two or three table-spoonsfuls, and stir in a half tea-spoonful saleratus, and drink while foaming.

277. SPRUCE BEER.

Allow an ounce of hops and half a table-spoonful of ginger to a gallon of water. When well boiled, strain it, and put in a pint of molasses, and half an ounce of the essence of spruce; when cool, add a tea-cupful of yeast, and put into a clean, tight cask, and let it ferment for a day or two, then bottle it for use. You can boil the sprigs of spruce instead of the essence.

278. TABLE BEER.

To eight quarts of boiling water put a pound of molasses, a quarter of an ounce of ginger, and two bay leaves; let this boil for a quarter of an hour, then cool, and work it with yeast, the same as other beer.

COOKERY FOR THE SICK.

COOKERY FOR THE SICK ROOM.

Too little attention is generally paid to the preparation of food for the sick, and when we consider that "kitchen physic is often the best physic," it is a matter of surprise that so important a subject should be so frequently neglected. The palate of a sick person is usually more nice, and less easily pleased than one in good health, and the utmost delicacy is required in preparing nourishing articles of diet.

The cookery for the sick room is confined to the processes of boiling, baking and roasting; and it may be useful to offer a few remarks upon the principles which render these processes serviceable for the preparation of food. By cookery, alimentary substances undergo a two-fold change; their principles are chemically modified, and their texture is mechanically changed. The extent and nature of these changes greatly depend on the manner in which heat has been applied to them.

279. BOILING.

Boiling softens the animal fibre, and the principles not properly soluble are rendered softer, and easier of digestion. In boiling meat, the water should be scarcely brought to the boiling temperature, but it should be long kept at a lower than the boiling point of water, or in that state which approaches more to stewing than to boiling. The nature of the water is also of some importance. Dr. Paris observes, that meat boiled in hard water is more tender and juicy than when soft water is used; while vegetables are rendered harder and less digestible when boiled in hard water.

280. BAKING.

Excepting in the **preparation of** light puddings, the process of baking is **inadmissible for** the sick.

281. ROASTING.

Roasting softens the tendonous part of meat better than boiling, and it retains more of its nutritious principles. Care should always be taken that the meat **be neither** *over* nor *under-done;* for, although in the latter state it may contain **more** nutriment, yet it will **be less** digestible on account **of** the density of its texture. It has of late years been **much** the fashion to regard under-done roasted meat as being well adapted for weak stomachs; but no opinion is more erroneous.

282. ARROW ROOT.

A tumblerful of this may be prepared in a few minutes. **Put** a tea-spoonful of powdered arrow-**root into a bowl, moisten** it with **a** table-spoonful of cold water, **and stir it till free** from grains; then pour on boiling water, stirring it all **the** time till it changes from a thick to a transparent substance; **a little lemon** juice and sugar makes this a delicious draught of thickened lemonade. Arrow-root, prepared with milk **instead** of water, is more **substantial food, and** may be seasoned with salt. It may be made **as thick as blanc-mange** and eaten cold with cream and sugar.

283. CALVES-FOOT BLANC-MANGE.

Put a set of calves' feet, nicely cleaned and washed, into four quarts **of water, and reduce it by** boiling **to one-quart;** strain it and set it **by to cool.** When cold, scrape of the fat, cut it out of the bowl, avoiding the settlings at the bottom, and put it to a quart of **new** milk, with sugar **to taste, and boil it a few** minutes. If flavored with cinnamon or **lemon-peel, do it** before boiling; **if with rose-**water, do it after. Boil ten minutes and strain it through a fine sieve, and **stir it till it cools.** An excellent dish for the sick or well.

284. BEEF TEA.

Take a piece of lean but juicy beef, wash it nicely and cut it up into pieces about an inch square, put these into a wide-mouthed bottle, and cork it up closely; then set the bottle in a pan of water, and boil it for an hour or more if you have time. In this way you will get the pure juice of the meat, undiluted by any water, and a smaller quantity will answer the purpose of nourishment.

Or, cut a pound of lean beef in thin slices; put it into a quart and half a pint of cold water; set it over a gentle fire, where it will become gradually warm; when the scum rises, let it continue simmering gently for about an hour, then strain it through a sieve or napkin, let it stand ten minutes to settle.

But to make beef tea, mutton broth, and other meat soups, the flesh should be put in cold water, and this afterwards very slowly warmed, and finally boiled. The advantage derived from simmering, — a term not unfrequent in cookery books,—depends very much upon the effects of slow boiling, as above explained.

285. CHICKEN JELLY.

A very young chicken will not yield any quantity of jelly; a full grown one is the best, but even an old fowl will do very well when no other can be obtained.

Break the bones of a full-grown chicken, and cut the fowl into pieces. Put it into a clean pan and fill it with water. After boiling the chicken gently for four hours or more, strain it through a jelly bag. Add a little salt but no other seasoning. When the liquid is cold, it should be a clear jelly. They may be boiled again and yield more jelly.

286. GRUEL.

Indian, rye, oat, rice, and wheat meal, are used for gruel. Wet two or three spoonsful with cold water, and stir it into a quart of boiling water, and boil until it is well cooked. Indian meal should boil full half an hour.

287. PEARL SAGO.

When a sick person is tired of slops, pearl sago boiled in

water till it cools to a jelly, may be used; it may be eaten with powdered loaf sugar and a little cream.

288. EGGS.

Weak persons may take eggs in the following manner:— Beat an egg very fine, add some sugar and nutmeg, pour upon it a gill of boiling water, and drink it immediately.

Or, an egg broken into a cup, or beaten and mixed with a basin of milk, makes a breakfast more supporting than tea alone.

Egg Gruel.—Boil a pint of new milk; beat two new laid eggs to a light froth, and pour in while the milk boils; stir them together thoroughly, but do not let them boil; sweeten it with the best of loaf sugar, and grate in a whole nutmeg; add a little salt, if you like it. Drink half of it while it is warm, and the other half of it in two hours. It is said to be good for dysentery as well as nourishing.

289. WATER GRUEL.

Mix with one spoonful of wheat flour, two of Indian meal, and cold water enough to make a thick batter. Stir it into a pint of boiling water, if the gruel is liked thick; if thin, into more water; boil about forty minutes, putting in a little salt, and stirring it frequently. Take it off the fire, and add a little salt and butter, and pour it on small pieces of toasted bread.

290. MINT, BALM, AND OTHER TEAS.

Put either the fresh or dried plants into boiling water, in a covered vessel, which should be placed near the fire for an hour. The young shoots, both of balm or of mint, are to be preferred, on account of their strong aromatic qualities. These infusions may be drunk freely in feverish and in various other complaints, in which diluents are recommended. Mint tea, made with the fresh leaves, is useful in allaying nausea and vomiting.

291. MUTTON BROTH.

Take a neck of mutton, cut it in pieces, reserving a good sized piece to serve in the tureen; put it into cold water enough to cover it, and cover the pot close; set it on coals until the water is lukewarm, then pour it off, and skim it well; then put it again to the meat with the addition of five pints of water, a tea-spoonful of rice or pearl-barley, and an onion cut up; set it on a slow fire, and when you have taken all the scum off, put in two or three quartered turnips. Let it simmer very slowly for two hours, then strain it through a sieve into the tureen; add pepper and salt to taste.

292. ARROW-ROOT CUSTARDS.

Four eggs, one dessert-spoonful of arrow-root, one pint of milk sweetened and spiced to taste.

293. ARROW-ROOT JELLY.

If genuine, it is very nourishing, especially for weak bowels. Put into a sauce-pan half a pint of water, a glass of sherry, or a spoonful of brandy, grated nutmeg and fine sugar; boil it once up, then mix it by degrees into a dessert spoonful of arrow-root, previously rubbed smooth with two spoonsful of cold water; then return the whole into the sauce-pan; stir and boil it three minutes.

294. A QUICK MADE BROTH.

Take a bone or two of a neck or loin of mutton, take off the fat and skin, set it on the fire in a small tin sauce-pan that has a cover, with three-quarters of a pint of water, the meat being first beaten and cut in thin bits; put in a bit of thyme and parsley, and if approved, a slice of onion. Let it boil very quick, skim it nicely; take off the cover, if likely to be too weak, or else cover it. Half an hour is sufficient for the whole process.

295. VEAL BROTH.

Put the knuckle of a leg or shoulder of veal, with very little meat to it, an old fowl, and four shank-bones of mutton, extremely well soaked and bruised, three blades of mace, ten pepper-corns, an onion, a large bit of bread, and three-quarts of water, into a stew-pot that covers close, and simmer in the slowest manner after it has boiled up and been skimmed; or bake it; strain and take off the fat; salt as wanted. It will require four hours.

296. BROTH OF BEEF, MUTTON AND VEAL.

Put two pounds of lean beef, one pound of scrag of veal, one pound of scrag of mutton, three ounces of pearl barley, sweet herbs and ten pepper-corns, into a nice tin sauce-pan, with seven quarts of water; to simmer to three or four quarts, and clear from the fat when cold. Add one onion, if approved, or the white part of leeks. Soup and broth made of different meats, are more supporting, as well as better flavored. To remove the fat, take it off when cold, as clean as possible; and if their still be any remaining, lay a bit of clean blotting or cap paper on the broth when in the basin, and it will take up every particle.

297. CALVES' FEET BROTH.

Boil two feet in three quarts of water to half; strain and set it by; when to be used, take off the fat, put a large tea-cupful of the jelly into a sauce-pan with half a glass of sweet wine, a little sugar and nutmeg, and heat it till it be ready to boil, then take a little of it, and beat by degrees to the yolk of an egg, and adding a bit of butter the size of a nutmeg, stir it altogether, but don't let it boil; grate a bit of fresh lemon peel into it.

298. CHICKEN BROTH.

Put the body and legs of the fowl, after taking off the skin and rump, into the water it was boiled in, with one blade of mace, one slice of onion, and ten white pepper-corns. Simmer till the broth be of a pleasant flavor; if not water enough, add a little. Beat a quarter of an ounce of sweet almonds with a tea-spoonful of water fine, boil it in the broth; strain; and when cool remove the fat.

299. TAPIOCA JELLY.

Tapioca, one pound; water, six pints. Put them together over night; next morning boil quite clear, and of a proper consistence, then flavor to taste.

MEDICINAL DEPARTMENT.

300. MEDICAL PREPARATIONS AND HERBS

AS EVERY FAMILY OUGHT TO KEEP ON HAND.

Castor Oil—Dose, for a child a year old, a tea-spoonful; for an adult, a table-spoonful. **Sweet Oil.** Syrup Squills —Dose for a child half a tea-spoonful. Paregoric—Dose for a child, from five to twenty drops. **Wine Ipecac—Dose** to act as emetic, fifteen drops, repeated every fifteen minutes till it operates; **for an adult, a tea-spoonful** repeated as above. Senna—Dose **for an adult, a** table-spoonful of the leaves, steeped. Camphor. Composition—Dose, **for** an adult, a tea-spoonful. Hot Drops—Dose, adult, a tea-spoonful. Ground Mustard. Rhubarb—Dose, an adult, a tea-spoonful of the powder. **Sage.** Thoroughwort. Catnip. Spearmint. Horseradish **leaves.** Pennyroyal. Valerian. Lobelia—Dose, adult, a tea-spoonful once in fifteen minutes, till it operates. Burdock leaves. Hoarhound. Yarrow.

301. POISON ANTIDOTES.

For Oil of Vitriol or Aqua-Fortis, give large **doses of** magnesia and water, or equal portions of soft soap **and** water.

For Oxalic Acid, give magnesia, or chalk and water.

For Tartar Emetic, give Peruvian bark and water, **or a** strong decoction of tea, until the bark can be had.

For Opium or Laudanum, give an emetic of mustard, and use constant motion, and if possible the stomach-pump.

For Lunar Costic, give common salt.

For Corrosive Sublimate, give the whites of an egg mixed with water, until free vomiting takes place.

For Arsenic, doses of magnesia are good, but freshly prepared hydrated per oxide of iron is better.

When bitten by a Rattle-Snake, apply salt and indigo to the place bitten as soon as possible. Make a tea of blue or white indigo violet, and drink freely. Bind the herbs on or above the wound to prevent swelling.

To cure the poison of ivy, chew freely and swallow limitedly, the leaves or green twigs of the white pine.

To cure the sting of a Bee or Wasp, apply at once strong potash water, if obtainable: else, saleratus.

A sure antidote against poison:—a large tea-spoonful of made mustard mixed in a tumbler of warm water, and swallowed as soon as possible. It acts as instant emetic, sufficiently powerful to remove all that is lodged in the stomach.

A poison of any conceivable description and degree of potency, which has been intentionally or accidentally swallowed, may be rendered almost instantly harmless, by simply swallowing two gills of sweet oil. An individual, with a very strong constitution, should take twice the quantity. The oil will most positively neutralize every form of vegetable, animal or mineral poison, with which physicians and chemists are acquainted.

HYDROPHOBIA.

A celebrated physician, having been exposed to hydrophobia by attending a patient who died of it, was one day suddenly seized with all the symptoms. He resolved to terminate his life by stifling himself in a vapor bath. Having entered one for this purpose, he caused the heat to be raised to 170 degrees Farenheit, when he was equally surprised and delighted to find himself free from all complaint. He left the bathing room well, dined heartily, and drank more than usual.

Since that time, he says he has treated in the same manner more than eighty persons bitten, in four of whom the symptoms had disclosed themselves, and in no case has he failed, except in the case of one child, who died in the bath. The same doctor relates the case of a French musician, who was bitten by a mad dog at the same time with many other persons, who all died of hydrophobia. For his part, feeling the first symptoms of the disease, he took to dancing night and day, saying he wished to die gaily; he recovered. Attention is drawn to the fact, that the animals in which madness is most frequently found to develope itself, are dogs, wolves and foxes, which never perspire.

ANOTHER.

A person, on being bitten by any rabid animal, should use the following remedies without a moment's delay. The place of the bite should be washed clean, (and cupped if convenient); then take nitrate of silver, (lunar caustic) and burn the wound out in a most thorough manner, so as to destroy the virus. Take large doses of salt and senna, (or other physic,) for a week or longer if necessary; keep the bowels open. If any symptoms of the disease should appear, take a thorough lobelia emetic, vapor baths and injections, every day for a week, or until the symptoms subside entirely.

302. TO RESTORE LIFE TO APPARENTLY DROWNED PERSONS.

Avoid all rough usage. Do not hold up the body by the feet, nor roll it on casks or barrels, or rub it with salt or spirits, or apply tobacco. Lose not a moment in carrying the body to the nearest house with the head and shoulders raised. Place it in a warm room if the weather is cold; if the weather is warm, have the windows open. Preserve silence, and positively admit no more than three intelligent persons. Let the body be instantly stripped, dried and wrapped in hot blankets, which are to be frequently renewed. Keep the mouth, nostrils and throat, perfectly free and clean. Apply warm, dry substances to the back, spine, pit of the stomach, arm-pits and soles of the feet. Rub the body with heated flannels, or cotton, or warm hands. Warm injections of salt and mustard, or of brandy and water, may be thrown up into the bowels, and stimulating vapors be applied to the nose. Attempt to restore breathing by gently blowing with the bellows, into one nostril, closing the mouth and the other nostril. Press down the breast carefully with both hands, and then let it rise again, and thus imitate natural breathing. Keep up the application of heat, continue the rubbing, increase it when life appears, and then give a tea-spoonful of warm water, or wine and water. Persevere for six hours. Send for medical assistance quickly.

303. CURE FOR THE EAR-ACHE.

Prepare a mixture of oil of sweet almonds and laudanum, and put it into the ear; or, apply a small poultice, in which is put a raw chopped clove of garlic; or, roast a small onion, and put as much of the inside into the ear as you conveniently can.

304. EPILEPSY.

Dr. Chapman, editor of the Westminster Review, has been proving an important discovery the past year, viz.: the cure of epilepsy, and many diseases hitherto deemed incurable, by means of the external application of ice and hot water, in India rubber bags, at various parts of the spinal cord, acting thus upon the sympathetic nerve, and through it upon the most important and vital regions of the body. Most of the worst and most inveterate feminine diseases have yielded to the new cure. The treatment is as simple as it is grand. Any one who is troubled with the pressure of blood on the brain, will find that by holding a bag of ice on the nape of the neck ten minutes, an equable flow of blood can be secured. Those who are troubled with habitual cold may find relief by applying ice to the small of the back. Seven hospitals are already under Dr. Chapman's practice, and as yet no one can bring forward an instance of failure.

305. RHEUMATISM.

Skim off from the top of a No. 1 mackerel barrel, a half

pint of oil, the best you can get, warm it, and on going to bed, rub it on the body or part affected, thoroughly, before a good fire. At the same time, drink some brandy, a strong dose of composition or cayenne, to prevent sickness at the stomach. Afterwards wrap the whole body in a warm woolen blanket for the night. In the morning, wash with warm water and soap before a fire, and afterwards with brandy or New England Rum. Be careful and not take cold. The operation is not so pleasant as could be wished, but one or two applications have affected perfect cures in many cases of long standing.

306. CANCER.

Place a piece of sticking-plaster over the cancer, with a circular piece cut out of the center, a little larger than the cancer, so that the cancer and a small circular rim of healthy skin next to it were exposed. Then a plaster, made of chloride of zinc, blood-root and wheat flour, was spread on a piece of muslin the size of this circular opening, and applied to this cancer for twenty-four hours. On removing it, the cancer will be found to be burnt into, and appear of the color and hardness of an old shoe sole, and the circular rim outside of it will appear white and parboiled, as if scalded by hot steam. The wound is now dressed, and the outside rim soon supurates, and the cancer comes out in a hard lump, and the place heals up. The plaster *kills* the cancer, so that it sloughs out like dead flesh, and *never grows*. The remedy was discovered by Dr. Fell, of London, and has been used by him for six or eight years with unfailing success, and not a case has been known of the reappearance of the cancer where this remedy has been applied.

307. CURE FOR THE ASIATIC CHOLERA.

The usual premonitory symptoms of this disease are looseness of the bowels (diarrhœa), with or without pain, and sometimes vomiting, which may be cured in ninety-nine cases out of a hundred if attended to in season, but if neglected may suddenly advance to a more dangerous stage and terminate fatally. Take paregoric, tincture of rhubarb, tincture of cinnamon, of each equal parts and mix together. Take

a tea-spoonful of this each hour until thoroughly physiced, or the diarrhœa is stopped. If it grows worse use camphor, laudanum, hot drops, and such powerful remedial agents as the case may require. For the spasms, dissolve one ounce of camphor in a pint of alcohol, and rub the patient smartly with a coarse flannel, wet with this mixture, or rub on any of the powerful external remedies of the day.

308. BLEEDING PILES.

Make a strong tea of yarrow, and drink freely; or, take a piece of garget-root about the size of a hen's egg, put it into a pint of boiling water, and let it steep a few hours, when cool, take from one to three table-spoonsfuls, as the stomach will best bear daily, before eating.

309. CHOLERA.

Rev. Dr. Hamlin of Constantinople saved hundreds of lives by the following simple preparation during the terrible raging of Cholera in that city a few years since. In no case did the remedy fail where the patient could be reached in season. It is no less effective in cholera morbus and ordinary diarrhœa. A remedy so easily procured and so vitally efficacious should be always at hand. An ordinary vial of it can be had for 25 cents or so, and no family should be without it over night. The writer of this received the recipe a few days since, and having been seriously attacked with the cholera morbus the past week, can attest to its almost magic influence in affording relief from excruciating pain. Its prompt application will relieve pain and presumptively save life.

Take one part laudanum. one part camphorated spirit, two parts tincture of ginger, two parts capsicum.

Dose—One tea-spoonful in a wine-glass of water. If the case be obstinate, repeat the dose in three or four hours.

310. REMEDY FOR DIPTHERIA.

The treatment consists in thoroughly swabbing the back of the mouth and throat with a wash made thus:—Table salt, two drachms; black pepper, golden seal, nitrate of potash, alum, one drachm each. Mix and pulverize, put into a teacup half full of water, stir well, and then fill up with good vinegar. Use every half hour, one, two and four hours, as recovery progresses. The patient may swallow a little each **time.** Apply **one ounce each of spirits** turpentine, sweet oil and aqua ammonia, mixed, every hour, to the whole of the throat, and to the breast bone every four hours, keeping flannel to the part.

311. CURE FOR CROUP.

As soon as the first symptoms are discovered, apply cold water suddenly and freely to the neck and chest with **a** sponge; then lay a cloth wet with cold water on the chest, and closely cover with cotton batting (nothing else will do as well), and the breath will be instantly relieved. Give the patient plenty of cold water to drink, **and cover it warm in** bed, and it **will sleep sweetly.** There is no danger of taking cold by the operation.

312. TREATMENT OF SPRAINS.

Give the part rest; apply warm fomentations. If inflammation set in, or a large joint be affected, put on leeches and cooling applications, which may be removed at intervals if necessary. When the inflammation subsides, use friction and stimulating liniments; bandage with flannel. If very severe, apply blisters, or poultices made of bread and vinegar and water.

313. BLEEDING AT THE LUNGS, OR SPITTING BLOOD.

To check the bleeding, let the patient eat freely of raw table **salt. Loaf** sugar and rosin, equal parts powdered, take **a** tea-spoonful four or five times a day; it will be found of great use. A tea made **of yarrow, is** very useful in this complaint. Choose a light diet, chiefly of milk and vegetables, and avoid **all hot** and stimulating drinks. A plaster compounded **of tar and** hemlock gum should **be worn upon** the side and **breast, if** the patient suffers pain.

314. BOILS.

Make a poultice of ginger and flour, and lay it on the boil; this will soon draw it to a head.

MISCELLANEOUS.

315. SUBSTITUTES FOR TEA.

The first young leaves of the common currant bush, gathered as soon as they put out, and dried on tin, can hardly be distinguished from green tea. The fine green leaves of the red raspberry, gathered in a fair day, and cured in an open, airy room are not inferior to the ordinary teas of China, and far more healthy. They should be gathered in September or October.

316. TO TAKE OUT INK, FRUIT SPOTS, AND IRON MOULDS.

On cotton goods and colored silks, spots of common or durable ink can be removed by saturating them with lemon-juice, and rubbing on salt, then putting them where the sun will shine on them hot, for several hours. As fast as it dries, put on more lemon-juice and salt. When lemon-juice cannot be obtained vinegar will do. Iron moulds may be removed in the same way. Mildew and most other stains can be removed by rubbing on soft soap and salt, and placing it where the sun will shine on it hot. Where soap and salt will not remove stains, lemon-juice and salt will generally answer. The above things will only remove stains in warm weather, when the sun is hot.

For fruit stains, let the spotted part imbibe a little water, without dipping, and hold the part at a proper distance over a bit of lighted brimstone. The sulphurous gas which is discharged soon causes the spot to disappear.

317. RED ANTS.

Place in a closet, or wherever they appear, a small quantity of green sage.

318. RATS AND MICE.

They can be very easily got rid of, if people will only use the means. Get live plaster of Paris and flour, mix them dry in equal quantities, lay it in dry places and sprinkle a little sugar among it. Both rats and mice eat ravenously, the plaster sets firm directly after it is moistened, becomes a lump inside of them, and kills to a certainty.

319. TO MAKE HENS LAY IN WINTER.

At any time when the hens cannot hunt bugs and worms to supply their demands for meat food, they should have bits of chopped liver or even boiled beef; but raw, fresh meat is best, fed with their corn or other grain.

320. BORAX.

The washerwomen of Holland and Belgium, who get up their linen so beautifully white, use refined borax as a washing-powder instead of soda, in the proportions of a large handful of borax powder to about ten gallons of boiling water; they save in soap nearly half. All the large washing establishments adopt the same mode. For lace, cambrics, etc., an extra quantity of the powder is used; and for crinolines (required to be made very stiff,) a strong solution is necessary. Borax being a semi-neutral salt, does not injure the texture of the finest linen.

321. GILT FRAMES.

Boil three or four onions in a pint of water. Then with a gilding brush do over your glasses and frames, and rest assured that the flies will not light on the articles washed. This may be used without apprehension, as it will not do the least injury to the frames.

322. TO PRESERVE FURS.

Wrap some cloves or peppercorns with them, and keep in a dry place.

MISCELLANEOUS.

323. HAIR WASH.

Get one ounce of borax, half an ounce of camphor, powder them finely, and dissolve them in one quart of boiling water. When cold the solution will be ready for use. Damp the hair with this frequently. It not only cleanses and beautifies, but strengthens the hair, preserves the color, and prevents early baldness.

324. REMOVING SUNBURN.

Take a handful of bran, pour a quart of boiling water on it, let it stand one hour, then strain. When cold put to it a pint of bay rum. Bottle and use it when needed.

325. VALUABLE DISINFECTANT.

One pound of green copperas, sulphuret of iron, costing eight cents, dissolved in one quart of water, and poured down a privy, will effectually concentrate and destroy the foulest smells. For water-closets aboard ships and steamboats, about hotels and other public places, there is nothing so nice to cleanse places as simple green copperas dissolved under the bed, in anything that will hold water, and thus render a hospital or other place for the sick, free from unpleasant smells. For butcher stalls, fish markets, slaughter houses, sinks, and wherever there are offensive putrid gasses, dissolve copperas and sprinkle it about, and in a few days the smells will pass away. If a cat, rat or mouse died about the house, and sends forth an offensive gas, place some dissolved copperas in an open vessel, near the place where the nuisance is, and it will soon purify the atmosphere.

326. TO WASH FLANNEL WITHOUT SHRINKING.

Make a strong suds and put in your flannel or white woolen stockings, while the water is boiling hot. Then squeeze and pound them with a pestle till the water is cool enough to put your hands to the work. You will find there is little need of rubbing. Rinse in water as hot as the hands will bear. If their is a little soap remaining in the rinsing water, it is all the better. The sooner they are dried, the less they will shrink. This method, from an old housekeeper, is sure to prove the right way, if strictly followed.

327. STARCH.

There is no better way for making nice starch for shirt bosoms, than to boil it thoroughly after mixing, adding a little fine salt, and a few shavings of a star or a spermaceti candle; the star or pressed candle, is quite as good as sperm. Let the starch boil at least ten minutes, and it will give a gloss, if neatly ironed, fully satisfactory to the exquisite taste of a dandy.

328. SCARLET ON WOOLEN.

For two pounds of goods take two ounces of cochineal, and two ounces of cream of tartar. Boil the dye fifteen minutes, then dip in the goods, and air till the color suits. Color in brass or copper.

329. TO REMOVE GLASS STOPPERS.

To remove a glass stopper, if fixed in a bottle so as not to be removed, pour a few drops of sweet oil around the same; set it in the sun, and it will soon work down and release the stopper.

330. TO SEASON NEW EARTHEN WARE.

Before using, place it in a boiler with cold water, and then heat it gradually and let it remain in till the water is cool. This will render it less liable to crack, especially if used for baking in.

331. TO CLEAN ALABASTER.

For cleaning alabaster, there is nothing better than soap and water. Stains may be removed by washing with soap and water, then whitewashing the stained part, letting it stand some hours, then rinsing off the whitewash and rubbing the part stained.

332. MARBLE STAINS.

Mix up very strong lees with quicklime, to the consistency of milk, put it on to the marble with a brush, leave it on for twenty-four hours, and afterwards wash it off with soap and water. Should this fail, the following may be tried:—

Take two parts of common soda, one part pumice stone, and one part finely powdered chalk; sift through a fine sieve, and mix with water. Rub it well over the marble, and wash with soap and water.

333. THE TEETH.

Every body admires a full, well-formed, and clean set of teeth. A handsome set of teeth is a passport to favor. To eat without sound teeth is next to impossible. They are essential alike to good looks and good living. Their usefulness and beauty are appreciated, but they are often neglected till decay begins its unwelcome inroads. The preservation of the teeth is a matter which should be carefully urged upon children and young people, because the causes of decay may generally be traced to a neglect of the teeth in the early period of life. The teeth may easily be kept clean and sound if a person enjoys fair health. They should be cleaned after every meal, in order to remove the particles of food that would otherwise be converted into acid, and act injuriously upon the enamel. No dentrifice is required. Pure water, neither hot or cold, but tepid rather, should be used, and the brush should be applied to the edges and inner side of the teeth, as well as to the outside. A wooden or quill tooth-pick (metalic ones are injurious) may be used to remove any particles of food clinging between the teeth. By this method they may be kept perfectly clean, and their soundness insured for a much longer period than is usually the case, while the unnecessary pain and expense occasioned by dental treatment may be avoided. Nothing either very cold or very hot should be allowed to come in contact with the teeth.

334. INK STAINS.

Ink stains may be removed from linen by dipping the spotted part into hot melted tallow; that of mould candles is best if made of ordinary tallow; composite candles will not answer the purpose. The linen may then be washed, and the spots will then disappear.

To take stains out of table-linen, if they be caused by

acids, wet the part, and lay on it some salt of wormwood; then rub it well, and afterwards rinse it in clean water. If the stains wine, fruit, etc., have been long in the linen, rub the part on each side with yellow soap; then lay on a mixture of starch in cold water, very thick; rub it well in, and expose the linen to the sun and air till the stain comes out. If not removed in three or four days, renew the process; keep the dressing moist by sprinkling it with a little cold water.

335. SCOURING KNIVES.

A small clean potato, with the end cut off, is a very convenient method of applying brick dust to knives, keeping it about the right moisture, while the juice of the potato assists in removing stains from the surface. A better polish can be got by this method than by any other, and with less labor.

One of the best substances for cleaning knives and forks, is charcoal, reduced to a fine powder, and applied in the same manner as brick dust is used. This is a recent and valuable discovery.

336. TO MEND CROCKERY-WARE.

One of the strongest cements and easiest applied for this purpose, is lime and the white of an egg. To use it, take a sufficient quantity of the egg to mend one article at a time, shave off a small quantity of lime and mix thoroughly. Apply quickly to the edges, and place firmly together, when it will very soon become set and strong. You will mix but a small quantity at once, as it hardens very soon so that it cannot be used. Calcined Plaster of Paris would answer the same purpose.

INDEX.

MEATS.

Selection of Meats	5
Beef	5
Mutton	5
Lamb	6
Pork	6
Venison	6
Bacon	8
Hams	6
Preparing Meats	6
To roast Beef	11
To roast Veal	12
To roast Mutton and Lamb	12
To roast Pork	13
Rolled Neck of Pork	14
To roast a Pig	14
To roast Venison	15
Boiled Beef	15
Beef A-la-mode	15
Stewed Beef Steak	16
Beef Steaks broiled	16
Beef, cold tenderloin	17
Beef, cold steaks to warm	17
Beef, minced	17
To stew a shoulder of Mutton	17
Mutton Chops	18
Sweet Bread, Liver and Heart	18
Minced Meat	18
Broiled Ham and Eggs	18
Boiled Ham	19
Pork Steak	19
To boil a leg of Mutton	19
Good pickling for Beef and Pork	19
Observations on Carving	19
Meat Broth	21
Beef or Mutton Soup	21
Sandwiches	21
Dried Beef	22
Sausages	22
Tripe	22

PICKLES.

Pickling	23
Cucumbers	23-24
Mixed Pickles	24
Cold Slaw	24
Pickled Tomatoes	24
Pickled Oysters	25

POULTRY.

Chicken Pie	26
Chicken Pot-Pie	26
Roast Turkey	27
Roast Ducks and Geese	27
Roast Chicken	28
Pigeons	28
Chicken Soup	28
Sauces for Game or Poultry	29

FISH AND OYSTERS.

New England Chowder	30
To fry Cod, or other Fish	30
To broil Shad	31
To fry Shad	31
Salmon	31
Boiled Salmon	31
Broiled Salmon	31
Broiled Fish	32
Salmon rolled	32
Fried Smelts	32
Clam Soup	33
Oyster Soup	33
To fry Haddock	33
Brook Trout	33
Dish of fried Cod	33
Cod-fish Cakes	33
Fried Shad	34
Salt Mackerel	34
Fresh Mackerel, soused	3

INDEX

Broiled Cod	34
Fried Cod	34
Salt Cod-fish	35
Dried Cod-fish	3
Stewed salt Cod	35
A dish of cold boiled Cod	35
Eel Broth	35
Stewed Oysters	35
Oyster Sauce	36
To fry Oysters	36
Fish Sauces	36

VEGETABLES.

Potatoes	37
Cooking Potatoes	37
Vegetable Soup	38
Brilla Soup	38
Soup	38
To dress celery	38
Drying Pumpkins	39
Green Peas	39
Onions	39
To cook Tomatoes	39
Green Beans	40
Sweet Corn	40
Baked Beans and Peas	40
Corn Oysters	40

BREAD AND BISCUIT.

White Bread	41
Indian loaf bread	41
Rye and Indian bread	41-43-44
Good brown bread	42
Brown, or Dyspepsia bread	42
Brown bread	44
Dyspepsia bread	44
Pumpkin bread	44
Sago bread	44
Cheap bread	44
Corn meal bread and cake	45
Rice bread	46
Scotch bread	47
Rye meal bread	47
Premium wheat and Indian bread	47
Rice bread and Muffins	47
Milk biscuit	47
Soda biscuit	47
Biscuit, or rolls	48
Arrow-root drops, or biscuits	48
Block Biscuits	48
Cinnamon Biscuits	48
Receipts for making yeast	48-49-50

PRESERVES AND JELLIES.

To preserve Barberries	51
Raspberry Jam	51-52
Peach Jam	52
To preserve Damsons	52
The Tomato as food	52
Tomato Catsup	53
Tomato Sauce	53
Tomato Figs	53
To boil Pears	54
To stew Pears	54
Preserved Pears	54
To preserve Grapes	54
Strawberry Jam	54
To preserve Quinces	54
To preserve Peaches, Plums, &c.	55
Scotch Marmalade	56
Honey Butter	56
Apple Butter	56
Currant Jelly	56-57
Rhubarb Jam	57
Apple Sauce	57
Apple Island	57
Orange Marmalade	58
Apple Jelly	58
To bake Apples	58

DESSERT AND SIDE DISHES.

Poached Eggs	59
To boil Eggs	59
Egg Omelets	59
Fruit Cream	59
Charlotte Russe	59
Blanc Mange	59-60
Brandy Peaches	60
Cup Custards	60
Orange Custards	60
Ice Currants	61
Icing for Cake	61
Ice Cream	61
Ice Cream, with fruit	62
Snow Cream	62
Cream Custard	62
Cherry Ice Cream	62
Currant Ice Cream	62
Fine Apple Cream	63
Lobster Salad	63
Asparagus and Eggs	63
Asparagus boiled	63

PASTRY. PIES.

Pie Crust	64
Plain Custard Pie	64
Rhubarb Pies	64
Custard Pies	65
Pumpkin Pies	65
Pigeon Pie	65
Oyster Patties	66
Potatoe Pie	66
Mince Pie	66-67
Lemon Pie	67-68
Mock Apple Pie	68
Squash Pie	68
Rice Pie	68
Tomato Pie	69
Peach Pie	69
Corn Starch Pie	69
Chicken and Turkey Patties	69
Apple Pie	70

INDEX.

Cherry Pie........................70
Whortleberry Pie.................70
Berry Pies.......................70
Small Puffs......................70
Washington Pie...................71
Cream Pie........................71

CAKES.

Rye Cake......................71–72
Corn Cake........................72
Corn Griddle Cake................72
Tea Cake......................72–73
Tumbler Cake.....................73
Sponge Cake...................73–74
Seed Cake........................74
Lemon Cake....................74–75
Queen Cake.......................75
Short Cake.......................75
Cold Water Rusk..................75
Pound Cake.......................76
Prairie Cake.....................76
Louisa Sponge Cake...............76
Loaf Cake........................76
Temperance Cake..................77
Indian Meal Puffs................77
Bread Cake.......................77
Rice Cake.....................77–78
Green Corn Cake..................78
Cookies..........................78
Jumbles..........................79
Washington Cake..................79
Buckwheat Cake...................79
Pan-cake.........................80
Indian Cake...................80–81
Hard Wafers......................81
Plum Cake........................81
Cream Cake....................81–82
Doughnuts.....................82–83
Apple Fritters...................83
Hoe Cake......................83–84
Crullers.........................84
Ginger-nuts...................84–85
Muffins..........................85
Gold Cake—Silver do..............86
Cocoa-nut Cake...................86
Oyster Corn Cake.................87
Western Cake.....................87
Common Cake......................87
Cider Cake.......................87
One egg Cake.....................87
Frosting for Wedding Cake........87
Gingerbread......................88
Pork Cake........................88
Harrison Cake....................88
Coffee Cake......................88

PUDDINGS AND SAUCES.

Observations on making puddings..89
Transparent pudding..............89
Cheshire pudding.................90
Tapioca pudding..................90

Quince Pudding...................90
Baked potato pudding.............91
Almond Pudding...................91
Custard Pudding..................91
Flour pudding....................92
Sago pudding.....................92
Boiled custard pudding...........93
Rice pudding..................93–94
Boston apple pudding..........94–95
Indian pudding................95–96
Lemon pudding....................96
Vermicelli pudding...............97
Suet pudding.................97–101
Spring pudding...................97
Batter pudding...................98
Bread pudding....................98
Christmas pudding.............98–99
Plum pudding.....................99
Rye pudding.....................100
Apple custard pudding...........100
Bird's nest pudding.............100
Berry pudding...................100
Cottage pudding.................101
English plain pudding...........101
Corn pudding....................101
Arrow root pudding..............101
Cracker pudding.................102
Cocoa-nut pudding...............102
Pine apple pudding..............102
Pudding Sauce...................102

DOMESTIC WINES AND FAMILY BEVERAGES.

Grape wine......................103
Currant wine....................103
Elderberry wine.................104
Rhubarb wine....................104
Cottage beer....................104
Ginger beer.....................105
Hop beer........................105
Mead............................105
Spruce beer.....................105
Table beer......................105

COOKERY FOR THE SICK.

Cookery for the sick room.......106
Boiling.........................106
Baking..........................107
Roasting........................107
Arrow root......................107
Calves-foot blanc-mange.........107
Beef tea........................108
Chicken jelly...................108
Gruel...........................108
Pearl sago......................108
Eggs, and egg gruel.............109
Water gruel.....................109
Mint, balm, and other teas.....109
Mutton broth....................109
Arrow root custards.............110
Arrow root jelly................110

INDEX.

Quick made broth.................110
Veal broth.......................110
Broth of beef, mutton or veal....111
Calves-feet broth................111
Chicken broth....................111
Tapioca jelly....................111

MEDICINAL DEPARTMENT.

Medical preparations and herbs, as every family ought to keep on hand......112
Poison antidotes.............112-113
Hydrophobia..................113-114
Drowned persons, to restore..........114
Ear-ache.........................115
Epilepsy.........................115
Rheumatism.......................115
Cancer 116
Asiatic Cholera..................116
Bleeding Piles...................117
Cholera..........................117
Diptheria, remedy for............117
Croup, cure for..................118
Sprains, treatment of............118
Bleeding at the lungs, to check..118
Boils............................118

MISCELLANEOUS.

Substitutes for Tea..................119
To take out ink, fruit spots, and iron moulds..........................119
Red Ants.........................120
Rats and Mice....................120
To make hens lay in winter..........120
Borax............................120
Gilt Frames......................120
To preserve furs.................120
Hair Wash........................121
Removing sunburn.................121
Valuable disinfectant............121
To wash flannel without shrinking....121
Starch...........................122
Scarlet on woolen................122
To remove glass stoppers.........122
To season new earthen ware.......122
To clean alabaster...............122
Marble stains....................122
The teeth........................123
Ink stains.......................123
Scouring knives..................124
To mend crockery-ware............124